LAST DORSET DIARIES

In memory of my parents
Alan John Ernest Edelsten
(January 15th 1907 – February 18th 1968),
Grace Eliott-Drake Edelsten
(June 24th 1908 – May 6th 2001),
and of their noble, war-tried generation and its values.

LAST DORSET DIARIES
On Dungeon Hill

DAVID EDELSTEN

HALSGROVE

First published in 2008 by Halsgrove
Text © 2008 David Edelsten

ISBN 978 1 84114 825 0

British Library Cataloguing-in-Publication-Data
A CIP data record for this book is available from the British Library

HALSGROVE
Halsgrove House
Ryelands Industrial Estate, Bagley Road,
Wellington, Somerset TA21 9PZ
Tel: 01823 653777
Fax: 01823 216796
email: sales@halsgrove.com
website: www.halsgrove.com

Printed and bound in Great Britain by
Cromwell Press Ltd, Wiltshire

FOREWORD

IMMEDIATELY after a cock pheasant calls his spring challenge there's a noise like a child thrumming his fingers on a balloon. It's the second part of the bird's display as it whirrs its wings, a visual and audible "keep out'" to rivals. And if you watch a trout rising, and study it carefully, you'll see it dimples, bulges or splashes the surface, depending on whether its hapless meal is a nymph, semi-emerged, or fully-winged fly.

You cannot see these unless you stop. Completely. But for most of us natural history is Attenborough and the dawn chorus sung by Orange and Blackberry, not greenfinch and blackbird. We are constantly wired, literally and emotionally, and stumble further down the 21st century seeking silicon-chipped solace.

Happily, our dogs and horses don't know this. They trust in our love, not the latest brand, and live at a pace guided by warmth of scent and hardness of ground. And if we stay beside and astride them, we can find a way back to the beauty of our countryside.

David Edelsten has never strayed from that path. Perhaps it's impossible for cavalrymen, always drawn to the sweetness of hay over the tang of diesel. Living in Dorset, in Hardy country, he knows old turf in winter and new cowslips in spring and adores them equally. He's passionate about the music of hounds and evensong (though the former, actually, might have the edge.). And he is wonderfully brigadierish when it comes to litter louts and urban absurdities that infect our lives.

Walking over the plough yesterday, I picked up a shepherd's crown, the local name for fossilised sea-urchins. It had lain there for millions of years before I popped it in my pocket. So much of our countryside is like that, just waiting to be discovered. David is a good guide to those with time to stop and stare.

Jonathan Young,
Editor *The Field*

INTRODUCTION

A NIMALS, I find, must either be everything or nothing in one's daily life. That is to say, if you keep animals, be they horses, dogs, or whatever is your fancy, you can never forget them, their needs rise and, you hope, go down with the sun every single day, and for as long as their sadly short lives overlap with yours. It's a benign tyranny, and a paradox: our domestic animals civilize us, make us human.

A perceptive friend, asked by my wife Diana for a *critique* of my second book, *More Dorset Diaries*, said, "I missed Perdita!" So do we miss the bewitching lurcher who was the heroine of *Dorset Diaries*. In her place I offer as a theme for this, I promise, the last in the series, our small family of horses Dandelion and Bluebell, progeny of a much-loved Irish mare called Daisy.

Since Dandy was foaled in our paddock here 17 years ago, and his full-sister Bella a year later, they have seldom been completely out of mind, and have shared countless hours of my life. If you will be so patient as to read that far, you will learn how, one dark February day, when the end of Dandy's working life lurched suddenly into view, the title and the idea of this book came to me. It is not, I hope, a gloomy book, and, as I sketched this Introduction, I fully intended to contrive a happy ending.

The other thread which I hope you may enjoy following is made up of the bits and pieces from a lifetime's reading and listening with which I have headed some of the sections, and dotted here and there in the text. They are no more than scraps from the ragbag of memory – 'Other Men's Flowers' as that great man Archie Wavell called his poetry anthology – but I have tried to match their various colours to their settings. Most of the quotations will no doubt be familiar, but I leave you to guess, should you need to, where each one comes from. It's intended as a game, but you don't have to play: if you want to cheat the answers are in the section I have called 'Ragbag' at the end!

These 'diaries' cover the better part of two years, more or less in sequence, with a date given where I have a note of it. But, every now and then, by way of diversion, I allow the odd bee to escape from under my bonnet, hoping that the buzzing won't annoy you.

Glanvilles Wootton, 2008

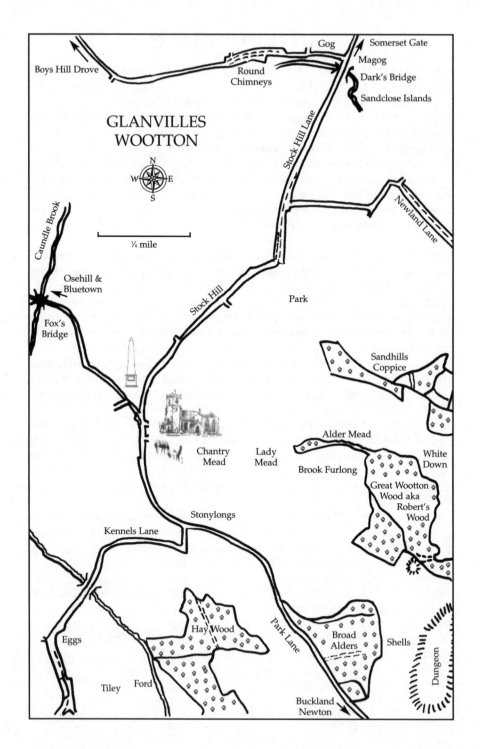

GLANVILLES
WOOTTON

N
W   E
S

¼ mile

Boys Hill Drove

Round
Chimneys

Gog

Somerset Gate

Magog

Dark's Bridge

Sandclose Islands

Stock Hill Lane

Newland Lane

Caundle Brook

Osehill &
Bluetown

Fox's
Bridge

Stock Hill

Park

Sandhills
Coppice

Alder Mead

White
Down

Brook Furlong

Great Wootton
Wood aka
Robert's
Wood

Chantry
Mead

Lady
Mead

Stonylongs

Kennels Lane

Hay Wood

Park Lane

Broad
Alders

Shells

Dungeon

Eggs

Tiley   Ford

Buckland
Newton

I

*"It was a spot which returned upon the memory
of those who loved it..."*

LET'S see... where were we when we last parted, said "Good night!" to each other, you and I? It was in Park Lane. Not in London – God forbid – but in the road, not much more than tractor-wide, that winds down off the shoulder of Dungeon Hill into our village.

I had ridden Bella up there early one August morning to look for hounds, and found them. Dungeon, or Donjon, you will remember was given its suggestive name by the Norman invaders a thousand years ago when they first stumbled on the great Iron Age fort that crowns it. It is the last outpost of the Dorset Downs, standing as it does, an island, in the extreme southern edge of the Blackmore Vale.

Our house is at the foot of the hill, next to the church, on the edge of the village now, though no doubt once in its centre, medieval villages having had a way of shifting to fresh, healthier ground. It was the Rectory, until my father bought it just after the war. It is L-shaped, a south-facing Georgian front stuck on a Tudor longhouse, with, its special charm, a straggle of characterful outbuildings, coach-house, stables, cowsheds and the like, at the back. I was a boy in this house before going for a soldier, and am totally, irremediably and fatally in love with the place.

Diana and I have between us four children, her two girls and my two boys, all in their forties now, six grandchildren, as already mentioned two horses, and a big gap where there used to be a dog. So much for 'the story so far'....

June 20th, 2006.

"What is this world? What asketh men to have?"

RODE Bella this morning, off the field. Had I been riding her brother Dandy I would have been obliged to bring them both into the stable, she creates such a fuss if left on her own. But Dandy is quite phlegmatic when I borrow his sister, just goes on grazing; this morning he didn't even bother to quit 'far guzzle', as I call the distant end of the field, when I found her, as I so often do, waiting for me almost at the gate.

He was neighing anxiously for us, however, when we returned. I fancy that horses always suppose that their world has come to an end when something untoward happens, they are like Chicken Licken, great fatalists, for ever supposing that the sky is about to fall on their heads.

You cannot saddle Bella quickly. If you do, being 'cold backed', she falls down, flat, suddenly, like a house of cards. So we walk along the lane, through the gate into my neighbour's field Stonylongs, before I can tighten her girth and climb aboard. Thankfully there are no grazing playful horses to avoid, Bella can be quite a handful among loose horses. There are just ewes with their now well-grown lambs, past the pretty stage but still fixated on mum and milk. They are all sitting in family blobs in the islands of shade cast by specimen park trees. It's hot, although the sun is barely up, but there are no flies yet, and a blackbird is singing – heaven really.

Off Stonylongs and on the road a tractor roars up behind us, out of view yet, but the row deafening... and threatening; it sounds like a Spitfire taking off. I spin Bella round to face it, as it powers into view. It is so much safer in the narrow confines of an overgrown summer lane to let her see the oncoming monster, and to urge her by it briskly so that our combined speeds make the hazardous moments of its passing as brief as possible.

Bella is quite unfazed but the driver looks chastened: we gave him a fright. His enormously long, rattling, hay-trailer is empty, and he is obviously running late. I have every sympathy, it's the time of year for hurry on the farm and for the rest of us, who merely live and play but do not work in the countryside, to look out for ourselves.

Only a few days before we had had a similar experience with a digger. First hearing it behind us, then spinning round to face what turned out to be an enormous yellow praying-mantis that quite filled the road. Yellow is not a horse's favourite colour, yellow and black together they can find quite threatening. Bella's mother once bolted with me when we were suddenly confronted by school bus with hornet stripes on its backside. But, as with the tractor, Bella was unperturbed, the perfect lady, and the plant operator likewise, was a perfect gentleman.

OFF THE road again, and we are following one of a pair of 'tramlines' through wheat. The corn stands about eighteen inches high, with here and there clumps of ryegrass left over from last year's crop standing twice as high above it. Do they 'rogue' ryegrass I wonder – do they in fact rogue at all these days? Our children used to earn useful pocket money roguing at harvest time in their school holidays, but I don't hear of or see it done now.

We turn at last out of the corn, where the horseflies are starting to get busy, into the grateful cool and shade of Hay Wood. We are on an egg-run, so, once through the wood and the ford beyond, I give her a burst across hay stubble whilst the satchel at my saddle-Ds is still empty. She romps joyously, such a bubbly ride, but, as we near the exit gate, I just say, ever so quietly, in her ear almost, "OK; OK; Bel-bells, well done!". Without so much as a touch of the rein she slows to a trot, then a walk.

At the poultry farm she stands untended, like a cowboy's quarter-horse, whilst I fill two egg-boxes and pay what is due. I give her the sugar lump that is still in my pocket, and which her brother would have had if he had bothered to come and greet me when I caught her. (This was probably a mistake, she will always expect one whenever we stop for eggs in future.)

I climb into the saddle again, using the mounting block kindly provided for us by the poultry farmers. It is an old milk stand, where the churns would have been put out daily for collection, a reminder of when we truly lived in what Thomas Hardy called the 'Vale of Little Dairies'.

Bella snatches an enormous mouthful of goose-grass, which trails around her feet as I let her slouch, munching, towards home. She's such a pet, and you can't hurry with a dozen eggs on board…. at least that was what I thought, but another racing tractor roared up behind us. I cantered her on to turn off the road back into Stonylongs, so that the driver needn't slow down.

It's not just a question of 'speed the plough', I also believe very strongly that riders on the public road are duty bound to be as helpful as possible to drivers of wheeled vehicles, and should be seen to be so. The tractor driver gave us a friendly and no doubt grateful wave as he sped past behind us.

ONCE home, by the magic of electronic mail, I asked two of our 'children' what they remembered of 'roguing'. If you want something in a hurry, ask a busy person… ; sure enough, within the hour came their answers. From Louise, my younger step-daughter, in Milan, mother of three smalls who has started up her own business, employing a dozen or so people, "roguing was hard and hot work with lots of cuts up my arms from the corn etc! Still I enjoyed the physical side, ie getting out into the open and working. But do you remember I got fired at the end, for gossiping too much? It was completely unfair of course!" Louise had been doing her A Levels at Sherborne Girls School at the time.

From Miles, at that same time at Sherborne Boys' School, my younger son and father of my grandson Othello, roguing meant "lacerated hands, blazing sun and aching feet… occasionally entering a trance state whereby it is difficult to remember which is the crop and which the rogue – enough to put you off farming for life….. sitting down and having a cold drink at the end of the day was however a mitigating moment of joy and conviviality".

Miles runs Associated Press's Television Bureau in Tokyo, his work involves racing round that hemisphere at no notice, collecting the news pictures that we see on our TV screens: he lives dangerously, sometimes much too dangerously for his father's peace of mind.

I WAS reminded of Miles's description of roguing that very afternoon, when scything the thistles in our five-acre field, Chantry Mead. Time was when June was thought too early for cutting thistles, 'Cut them in June and it's too soon, cut them in July and they're sure to die' our old gardener used to say, but that was before global warming.

It's heavy work, scything thistles – rewarding, because every year there are fewer and fewer of them – but, like Miles roguing, it was all too easy to slip into a sort of catalepsy, and to be almost overcome by the wish not to see thistles. An hour of it was quite enough; I planted out baby leeks until weariness drove me indoors.

It had been a long day. On the previous evening I had given a talk to the 'Friends of Sherborne Library'. They could not have been a kinder or more attentive and appreciative audience, but I find such occasions intensely stressful. "Don't do it!" Diana always pleads when such an invitation comes in, knowing what a tizz it will put me in, but I feel obliged to accept if people are so kind as to ask me. Vanity no doubt comes into it too.

The result as always was that I went to bed with my mind racing, couldn't sleep, and was up with the sun, hoping to see the fox cub that she had spotted two morning before picking over the good things on the compost heap.

It was just as well that I had kept to myself the belief that it was in fact the gamekeeper's ginger cat Toffee that she had seen – a solitary cub of the size she described seemed so unlikely. However, a well-chewed pineapple top, emptied as you might empty half an orange of its flesh, was clearly the work of a fox. Next day it had returned and cleaned out the whole rotten heart of the inedible pine itself, but I never actually saw the cub.

June 23rd.

IT'S time you met Jasper. My step-grandson, now aged eight, he spends quite a bit of time with us. We are great buddies, he and I; our current project is a tree house that we are building in the orchard.

He is extraordinarily precocious socially, much more at ease with the world than I am, and, though a touch dyslectic.... or perhaps **because** he is a touch dyslectic.... he is incredibly sharp, observant, articulate, likeable and bright.

The other day, when I took him to Olivers, the favourite coffee spot in Sherborne, the lady behind the counter, very kindly lent over and asked "would the little man perhaps like a Coke?". "I'll have a *café latte* please" Jasper replied coolly, unbelievably London-y and grown-up.

And, when we had taken our high stool seats at the great plank table, which was a butcher's counter when I first knew it, he turned to me with a shrewd look, and, I think to put me gently in my place, said in a voice for all to hear "My Daddy's older than you are!".

I am not sure what the other customers made of it. We all eavesdrop at Olivers, leastways I do.

BELLA and I do an egg-run, anticlockwise. No eggs to collect this time but two notes to deliver – 'h-mail' I call it – for those in the parish whom I cannot reach via my computer.

It's always a bit nerve-wracking getting to within reach of letter boxes with a horse, usually at full extent of the reins under a porch, with various ornamental obstacles, not to mention tasty looking flowers that must not at any cost be browsed.

Then there is the possibility of Bella disgracing us both. The strange situation of being on a gravel drive or in a garden is scarcely calming to equine nerves; indeed she had her tail slightly raised as I hustled her safely away from our first call.

The text I was delivering, which was a day or so old, read…

"With the world and his wife coming here next Saturday it seems a good moment to THANK everybody for their efforts in keeping the Parish litter-free, and to beg everyone to keep up the good work. It is particularly important now with the Council verge cutters chopping every neglected piece of rubbish into a hundred pieces! I am sure that you will have noticed the difference since we started GWALB, and have seen from the Benefice Newsletter that the idea has caught on elsewhere."

… the rather inelegant acronym stands for Glanvilles Wootton Against Litter Bugs: more about that another day.

June 24th.

THE morrow was, as you have perhaps guessed, the day of our Church Fête. It was a completely breathless twelve hours, without any punctuation to speak of, certainly no full-stops, and it went something like this…

… cut flowers first thing for Diana's arrangement in the church, air dog before it might lift its leg in the spare bedroom (Jasper and his mamma, and a little caramel coloured Lucas terrier called George, the last-named unexpected and unannounced, had arrived the night before), take flower-arrangement to the church and arrange it tastefully in the squinny (a sort of serving hatch between the chancel and the Lady chapel), hang out washing, make the first of six visits to the horses to see if I can shut them out of the corral and sign it up for parking (I can't, with animals' unfailing instinct for doing the opposite of what is wanted

they are in the corral shelter, seeking sanctuary from the flies, I haven't the heart to shift them), mend toy for Jasper who tells mother, with a big wink at me, that I have broken it, cut lettuce (as ordered) and wash it, take cakes for Fête teas to Church Farm, commiserate with neighbour at Church Farm, who hosts the Fête in his garden, visit horses, again, and again, and again (see above), dig and bundle broccoli plants for sale, wheel-barrow them, along with two young Judas trees, round to the Fête site … such a happy scene, everybody turning out to do their bit as always in this village, the weather promising to be perfect… *receive a 'phone-call, Diana & Co stuck in Castle Cary, doing a recce on Melanie's new house, won't be back before the Fête kicks off, I'm to take her place helping with the teas, get myself a beer, discover toad that has gallantly made it to the top of the cellar steps has met a grisly end being squashed, fortunately fatally, under the opening door, remove it to the compost heap, get self lonely lunch, bring in horses who are still in shelter, tormented by clegs (horseflies), dangerous in their angry haste and body-language, though they usually come in lamblike, nearly get squashed between their churning shoulders and trampled under foot* (seriously, my day nearly ended there, but I get away with it), *sign parking, shift dung, sprint down drive to shut gate to stop lost souls roaring up it, get myself over to Church Farm kitchen to take up duty at the seat-of-custom receiving money for the teas, 'little grey cells' much stressed working out the change due on tea or coffee 50p, squash 40p, cake £1 a slice…* Sherborne Town Band is playing, it's a very, very happy, busy couple of hours, I greet and am greeted by innumerable friends, … *cash-up (£257.90, out of a total take of £1675 we later learn), get permission to quit my post, drift around a bit amongst the throng, nip into church to check the exact year of my father's death on his memorial, being ashamed to have forgotten it when asked by a reminiscing neighbour, check the car park several times until it is empty, put the horses out, collapse on the lawn bench, only to be importuned by George, the Lucas terrier, whom, on my return from the Fête, I found on the kitchen table, he rushes up to me with a yellow post-it stuck to his beard, one of many that Diana puts on the table to remind me of things that need doing, it reads 'check Landrover oil and tyre pressures', that will have to wait whilst I hand my brain over to be massaged by a crossword puzzle…*

THE word *Fête* is something of a curiosity. Presumably it is shorthand for a *Fête Champêtre*, like the one described with such charm by Anthony Trollope in 'Barchester Towers', at the crux of the novel. As a money-raising affair today a *Fête* has become a thing quite different. I find myself wondering when the word and the ideas that go with it were imported across the Channel, was it a nostalgic echo of pre-revolutionary France, Fragonard, Marie Antoinette and Co?

People round here used to pronounce the word 'feet': they don't any longer, the BBC has seen to that. "Did ye go to the Village *Feet*, Maister David?" old Tom, my father's groom/gardener would ask me. It is almost unimaginable today, the long ago immediately post-war world in which a man in his fifties or sixties would address the twelve-year-old son of his employer with such formality and 'respect'. In another typical, broad Dorset locution he used to refer to my sister in the third person as 'the little maid'.

Tom himself was a cross-channel import, or rather his name was – I won't give it here, it occurs too often in the local telephone directory – it was Anglo-Norman. But the man was Dorset, generations deep, the last person whom I can remember speaking its language regularly to me, and using no other. He had been in the trenches in World War I with a battalion of the county regiment, remembered Thomas Hardy, shared his birthplace, but had not a word of good to say of him.

My mother would have it that Tom was of gipsy extraction. Though he had settled kin around he was himself rootless and roofless, having neither house nor wife as long as I knew him. Presenting himself for employment within days of our settling in Buckland Newton, the next village to here, in 1945, he lodged locally, shifting lodgings when we moved.

He attached himself to us; in a sense I think we were his family – I am ashamed to reflect that I did not like him better, was not more attentive and kind to him, or take more notice of him when, old and worn out, he retired to the modern equivalent of the workhouse in Sherborne. I should have looked him up, and made a fuss of him, when I was home on leave.

One of the most telling stories of my mother's about Tom was of how she was talking to him one day as he dug the vegetable garden, when his fork turned up an old coin. "In a twinkling" my mother would say, "sharp as that! He put his boot on it, thinking I hadn't seen it". It tells you as much about my mother and her generation as it does about Tom, that the coin ended up in her specimen cabinet.

How I wish that I had made more of old Tom, sat at his booted feet in the saddle room when he was having a brew-up at the coke stove, learnt all that he could have told me about his childhood, schooling and war service, of Thomas Hardy, and now long-forgotten Dorset. Too late now, for this apology of a memorial, but – "Yes, Tom, I did go to the Fête: I'll tell you all about it".

June 25th.

SUNDAY, and Jasper comes with me to church. We have a problem persuading the irrepressible and squirming terrier George that he is not to be one of the party. It's lucky Jasper is in his combat kit as the orchard is a minefield – the seven rams who summer there have sewn anti-personnel mines all the way up the path (ram's poo on the soles of shoes is not welcome in the house). We survive, but Jasper has a stone in his sandal, and hops the last few yards through the graveyard, into church and all the way up to our front pew. His mother joins us during the opening hymn.

During the gospel reading Jasper sidles up to me in the pew and whispers, very seriously in my ear "Has Perdie got a grave?" – such things really worry children – Perdita was our late adored lurcher. I whisper back that she was cremated. He conveys this important intelligence to his mother in the same stage whisper, and then settles down with a dinosaur book during the sermon. But, as always, he comes up to the altar to kneel between us to be blessed.

After lunch they all go away, Diana en route for Italy to inspect Louise's new house in Milan: I am to be on my own, for four days, I hate it. The eternal pessimist, I think, as she is driven off, "Is that the last time I will see her alive?"; and when I have her on the answer-phone, "Is that the last time I will hear her voice?". I'm every bit as chicken-licken as the horses really.

"Allone, with-outen any companye".

II

*"Or ever… the pitcher be broken at the fountain,
or the wheel broken at the cistern…*

IF DANDY has been a bit slow in getting properly onto the page it is not because I don't still ride him – I do, just about every other day – but because his future has become rather clouded.

On a black day, back at the end of February, he suddenly stopped jumping. For some years now, through the hunting season, I have kept an old five-bar gate propped up in the paddock to pop him over on the day before taking him out with hounds, just to make sure that we were both still in full working order. It's a stout, no-nonsense jump, he knows it if he hits it, but it is no more than three feet high, nothing like the formidable obstacle that a hanging gate can be, but, jumping it 'cold' seemed a good enough test of his continued gameness and my ageing nerve.

We were due out with the South Dorset on the following day, so on this, as I say, black Monday, for the first time in all our years together, home from work on Dungeon Hill, he waltzed towards the familiar gate in his usual confident style, ears pricked, all smiles, but then, in the final stride, suddenly dropped anchor instead of taking off. I felt despair, could have wept almost, actually hid my face in my hands on the crest of his mane.

It was in that moment that the idea of this book was born. But don't think that I am going to go on in a pessimistic vein, as it happens, and as you shall learn, some nice surprises were waiting, just around the corner. But at that moment it was as if a theatre orchestra had struck a sonorous minor chord at the lifting of the curtain on a final act, of *Carmen* perhaps. All of a sudden the future looked a bit bleak, the dreaded step was to be heard for the first time on the stair; when would I hear the latch lift?

DANDY had previously given me notice, a fortnight before, had I not been wilfully blind to it. The last time out, after a memorable meet marking the first anniversary of the enactment of the asinine 'hunting-with-dogs' law, at Dewlish House, he had put a stop in at a familiar tiger-trap at the bottom of Dewlish Hang. A 'tiger trap' is a timber jump with an inviting triangular cross-section: despite the alarming name it is just about the easiest and most inviting obstacle that you are likely to meet out hunting.

Then he clouted the next jump with his front legs. This was a good stout straight-up-and-down post-and-rails, he barely kept his feet on landing. It was un-nerving: I took him home. It's neither fun nor sense riding a horse that isn't looking with proper respect at its fences. But I drew the wrong conclusion. Dandy is moody by nature, one horse on one day, a quite different horse on another, and I supposed that he was just having a bad day.

After that Black Monday I started to take a closer notice of his gait. He has one front foot much larger than the other, and has never been completely even at the trot, is happier cantering when he can favour one diagonal, prefers soft to hard gound, and hates going downhill. His rather indifferent, shallow-soled feet seem to me to be finding him out with age, the complex joints inside the hoof perhaps affected by arthritis; he probably wouldn't do for another hunting season.

Whilst I was digesting this unpalatable fact, invitations came in to take the last day of the season with two neighbouring hunts. Under the circumstances I had no choice but to ask that they mount me: I was to have two of the best days out with hounds that I can remember.

FOR THE day with the Blackmore & Sparkford Vale I asked also that they provide me with a pilot who would keep me with hounds without my having to face any of their enormous hedges: I don't pretend to cross the vale as I used once to, timber I don't mind, but blind hedges are a young man's game. The day had a magic quality, as I later wrote…

"Throughout the afternoon, except for one brief flurry of snow, the sun shone. And all day, almost from the moment we cleared Old Park Wood above Sherborne Castle, Dungeon Hill and behind it the Dorset Heights, the skyline that has meant home to me since boyhood, was in full view to our south, with, at one stage, hang-gliders spectacularly tipping themselves off the top of Batcombe Hill. Looking back I think that, all in all, it was one of the happiest days I have spent following hounds."

ON THE following Saturday, the Cattistock gave me as good a horse to ride as I have ever sat on. We were on turf and jumping timber all morning, I felt a boy again, this time with the full thrill of riding properly to hounds. Here is part of how I described that day …

"I DON'T know how it is, age I suppose, but the Hunting Bill seems to have affected my eyesight, and I couldn't tell you exactly what was going on up ahead. Anyway, my hands were full, I had enough to think of looking to myself. Softy took a generous hold – not too generous, just what I like. 'Here we go, I understand this business as well as you do, and am used to being up with hounds if you don't mind' he seemed to say. I let him get on with it.

Picking a fence I liked the look of to get started, soon it was ping, ping, ping – I haven't jumped so much for ages, or enjoyed myself more. To start with they were the usual half-round-larch hunt jumps. But number six was very no-nonsense, stand-up, stare-you-in-the-face, square sawn timber, with a drop (glad it wasn't number one) – ping again – number seven ditto, but up-hill.

We were off Melbury Park now, south over the Holywell-Evershot road. There was some plough, and a bit of puffing coming from the engine-room (Softy was past twenty years of age Huntsman Charlie Watts had said when he handed the horse to me) eight, nine, ten… lose count. Will you believe me if I tell you that I have never had a happier half hour with hounds, or had a mount more to my taste; and the sun was shining? (Would they sell me Softy – in my dreams!?)."

… you will also perhaps gather how a hunting correspondent, or this one at least, contrives to continue plying his trade without raising awkward questions as to the legality of what he was writing about. I should say that throughout the length of that season the Cattistock had been scrupulous in trying to observe the idiocies imposed on them by the new law, and indeed had actually seen off a legal challenge in court. They had followed trails unselfishly laid by my old friend Lucy Pinney, then one of the Masters of that hunt; her mother and I had been in the Pony Club together.

ONE final word about hunting before I leave the topic… for a month or so, at least. It doesn't do to be complacent about how the sport survived the first season after the ban, far less does it do to crow about it, but here is a simple, sober comment that bears on the topic, it comes from a report I had written a couple of weeks earlier on a day with the Quantock Staghounds…

"There was a wonderful turnout at the meet in the grass car park at Seven Mile Stone. Half term had brought out a lot of children to swell the large mounted field, and there was the usual army of foot-soldiers. In common with hunts all across the country this season, the Quantock would like to record their profound gratitude to Tony Blair for being such a good Recruiting Sergeant for their sport."

… from all that I saw and heard, hunting was never so popular in recent times, nor more strongly followed, than it was in the season of 2005-2006. I think that we ought to put up a statue to the great man, at Peterborough.

June 29th.

ON THE day of Diana's return from Italy I was housebound. Mr Sargent, who these many years has been doctor to this house's ills – I mean done all the painting, decorating and repairs – was making good an attic window, a single, round cyclopean eye installed by my father high up in the blind west gable wall. As it turned out the frame had rotted quite to bits, there was nothing for it but an eye-patch for the present: the window would require scaffolding and goodness knows what expense in joinery to replace.

I must be about the place in case an extra hand were needed, and to try to answer the questions that would normally be put to the Clerk of Works, the mistress of the house – I don't generally meddle with indoor things. So it seemed a good day to get the vet to give the horses their tetanus injections: vets, like doctors, are not always in command of their time, and one never quite knows exactly when they are coming; they too have to be waited on.

When she had, manfully, done the injections – Dandy is quite dangerous with vets and needles, the old softy becomes suddenly violent, lethal – I asked her to give me an opinion on his soundness. "What's the problem?" she asked; "You tell me" I replied unhelpfully, determined to get my money's worth, "I'm not giving you any clues".

I led him what I thought was a generous distance down the drive, turned him to trot him back, but she called "Further please!": she was taking no chances. I did as asked, then trotted him up to her, careful to leave his head entirely free, and to keep out of her line of sight. "There's nothing much, but he wallows a bit" she said, "seems slightly to favour his right front foot", (in other words throw his weight onto the left [near] fore, his larger foot).

It was a skilful observation, by a girl who was I guess somewhat younger than either of my stepdaughters, and was entirely accurate in my view, well worth the ten guineas or whatever that it will cost. She spoke of giving him 'bute', the pain-killing drug that can extend a horse's working life, but I don't think that would be much fun for either of us. He's pretty headstrong as it is, I wouldn't fancy my chances of stopping him if he couldn't even feel my hand on the reins.

Dandy's future remains clouded, I shall do nothing in a hurry: let's see how well we both summer.

July 1st – 3rd.

"WHERE are we having breakfast?" I sarcastically enquire when Diana breaks the news to me that we are invited out to lunch and supper on the following day. Very wisely, she doesn't usually disclose the contents of the diary more than a day or so in advance, she keeps it in shorthand so that I cannot read it. It's Saturday morning, and we are on our way to Beaminster, to hear Melvyn Bragg give an address about his latest publication, *Twelve Books That Changed the World*. It is in St Mary's church, where Tess's father-in-law was priest,

I am, privately, a touch sceptical about the outing. It is not his fault, but Lord Bragg is a 'celebrity', a category that fills me with distrust, although I wouldn't mind in the least being a celebrity myself. He is a Labour Peer – 'nuff sed' – and Diana once sat next to him at a dinner party when I wasn't present; he made a big impression and I am mildly jealous of him.

But it must be allowed that he is sound on the hunting issue, and that his weekly wireless programme, 'In Our Time', is the best broadcasting of the week. He gives a brilliant address, many of his choices being correct, and making a clever and amusing case for the more idiosyncratic selections, such as 'The Rules of Football'.

Before we left home, Neil, the young farmer whose rams are in the orchard, and who farms our grass, had arrived to mow the few acres we have 'up for hay' this year. It is scorching weather, and he is busy turning the rapidly drying crop when we get home. He is turning it for a second time at tea time, whilst the rest of the world is watching England lose to Portugal in a quarter-final of the World Cup, leaving no doubt as to where the priorities in his busy life lie.

Neil is a good stockman, you only have to see him with his rams to know that. He is quiet, speaks to them gently, lovingly almost, as if they were his children. It is I suppose no surprise that, although he is no horseman, he never asks me for help managing the horses, who must be juggled out of their shelter, and off a favourite bit of ground, before he can get access to the section of our meadow where he has to work. He just has the knack of handling animals.

As we leave for lunch on Sunday he is turning the hay for a third time, and as I am dressing for the evening's entertainment I hear the emphatic tunk-tunk-tunk of a baler at work in the paddock. From a window I see him leap from the tractor with which he is raking the hay into ridges, and run in giant strides to kick a stray heap into the path of the baler, so that not a bit of the crop be wasted. By hard physical work and dedicated single-mindedness, he has made what looks and smells like a good crop of meadow hay inside two days: he was to be heard carting the bales away at daybreak next morning.

Sunday's newspaper however carries a dire full-page report in which Sir Stuart Hampson, President of the Royal Agricultural Society of England, was quoted as saying that "Farming is close to being lost for ever": it makes me feel that we are on the edge of unimaginable waste and tragedy. But, as Oliver Goldsmith had it…

> "… times are altered; trade's unfeeling train
> Usurp the land and dispossess the swain"

… I take some comfort from the thought that we have been here, many times, before.

THE *Today* programme this morning carried an item about the proposed erection of a stair-lift on Dartmoor's Haytor; for me this was something of a dream come true. I have for some years now nursed a comic daydream in which Disabled Access to Public Footpaths Over Farmland, DAPFOF for short, becomes government policy. A 'tsar' is of course appointed, our Prime Minister, dewy eyed and lip aquiver, broadcasts to the nation about it, promising that the wonderful new policy is soon to be 'rolled out'.

How I loathe that tendentious expression, 'rolled out', suggesting as it does smooth well-oiled efficiency when you know that, whatever the latest vote-catching scheme might be, it will limp forth in the usual expensive, spavined fashion, escorted by thousands of newly appointed feather-bedded bureaucrats, tripping over themselves and getting in each others' way.

As my daydream unfolds, we learn that farmers and landowners, New Labour's kulaks, are to be fined enormous sums, perhaps put in prison, if they do not immediately level stiles or erect ramps over them.

How very often it is that the day's news trumps the most far-fetched parody!

❧

RIDING down off the hill on the Monday morning, patrolling my 'pitch', I found a small football favour discarded in the verge, no doubt at about 6pm on the previous evening when England failed in the World Cup penalty shoot-out. It is a St George's cross on a cardboard shield, about the size of a blazer badge, with the word England emblazoned across the top. It has an elastic band attached, and I ride home with it dangling from my wrist.

It has found a home on the kitchen dresser, decorating the belly of a George III silver tankard: I rather fancy it. There has been a lot of argument in recent weeks about people flying St George flags on their cars. The horses certainly don't approve, normally bombproof in traffic, they jump at the strange fluttering things. But I like to see displays of national pride: I'm all for flags, so long as they are not pale blue with a ring of stars on them.

The long, eventful weekend saw Diana away again, this time in London for Jasper's school play. I worked late into the evening cool, planting out the last of the leeks. For the first time there was no blackbird singing, from now on we have just to rely on the faithful robin and the tireless ringdove for outdoor music.... and the best of the roses are over. Oh dear!

"Janet! Donkeys!..."

GWALB stands, as I have already mentioned, for Glanvilles Wootton Against Litter Bugs, it's my invention, and I am very proud of it, it came about like this....

I don't in the least mind being thought eccentric, like David Copperfield's Aunt Betsy, who wouldn't allow a donkey to set foot on the green outside her cottage. In fact I regard it as an accolade, a mark of distinction in a world gone me-me-mad: anyway, every proper Englishman has a touch of Don Quixote in him. For as long as I can remember I had been conducting a one-man crusade against the rubbish that people leave in our lanes.

Then one day, as they say, I 'flipped'. Off my tall horse for the umpteenth time to pick up some revolting piece of litter, I determined to enlist allies. Greatly daring, as ever scared of being thought 'the bossy brigadier', and having consulted the rector, as one must before taking any important step, I put a circular appealing for help through every letterbox in the parish. (A copy of it is at the back of this book in case you care to read it).

The response was, almost without exception, warm and positive – "Thank you; yes, let's do it!" was the general tone of the replies. I found that I had been pushing against an open door.

We divided the parish into 'Pitches A-L', each pitch being a stretch of one of the roads that radiate from the centre of the village, with two or three families responsible for each pitch. The result has been a transformation, and so pleasing. Of course rubbish is still dropped by feckless people, but it doesn't lie there for long: ours must be one of the cleanest parishes in all Dorset.

"... perchance to dream..."

IT'S a big mistake, in my opinion, yet quite a common one, to suppose that your dreams can be of any interest to other people. I don't intend to make that mistake here, but I do believe that the subject of dreams, where they come from, what they mean, fascinates just about everybody. We all dream, surely, and most of our dreams, equally surely, leave us guessing.

Two of the books that my father put my way when I was still a schoolboy were John William Dunne's *An Experiment With Time*, and *The New Immortality*, books that evidently made a big impression on his generation but which I doubt that anybody reads today.

Dunne, who died in 1949, advanced the theory, half tongue-in-cheek I suppose, that time was somehow circular, dreams were prophetic, useful. One ought to make a careful note of them in the moment of waking, before they fled the memory for ever, keep writing material by your bed for that purpose.

An impressionable teenager, I swallowed Dunne's theories whole, did exactly what he advised about recording my dreams, kept it up for at least a fortnight, and then forgot about it, more-or-less, until today. I have no idea where those two books have got to, it's not like me to lose a book.

Perhaps my father claimed them back. If so they will have disappeared with much of the rest of his library when some sharp-eyed biblio-shark preyed on my mother shortly after his death, emptying his priceless shelves for a pittance, whilst I was away with my regiment, and she imagined herself to be short of money.

"Nothing can be made out of nothing."

MY OWN theory is that, just as 'matter is indestructible', or, to cite another of Dunne's titles, *Nothing Dies*. It seems to me that all our ideas, notions, inspirations even and dreams, must come from somewhere, be based on something seen or heard. Dreams must have causes, it is just that we cannot fathom them.

My childhood dreams, much like those of most children I suppose, were full of terrors, pursuit, flight, and, oddly enough, the ability to fly but somehow failure to take off, being anchored to the ground, when the need arose. Unlike Agatha Christie who, as I read in a recent biography of her, was haunted by nightmares well into her adult life, nearly unhinged by them in fact, my childish night fears were soon left behind.

Now, in old age, dreamless sleep is unknown to me. I always dream, but I look on my dreams as friends, as offering an escape from sleeplessness. Should I wake, and wish to sleep again, by asking myself "Where was I?", rather as you might look for your place in a book, I find that I can usually think myself back into my unfinished dream. It's a great comfort.

Sometimes a dream recurs in daylight, is 'broken' as we say by some sight or happening. But I couldn't begin to tell you what most of my dreams are made of, or how they are constructed, they seem to have a language and imagery of their own. Try to get your hands on a dream, to hold it and examine it, and, with a flick of its tail, it darts back into the dark unfathomable pool of the subconscious.

"... those wild regions of obscurity which are vaguely felt
to be compasing us about in midnight dreams of flight and disaster".

III

*"Every man thinks meanly of himself for not having been
a soldier, or not having been at sea".*

SAM Johnson was of course exaggerating to make a point, as he so often did, but I think we know what he meant: there is something undeniably admirable about the profession of arms, despite its necessary roughness, a unique virtue in it. Who knows anyone who didn't come out of the Services better than he went in: who doubts that it would be a wonderful thing for the youth of the country, if only it were feasible, to re-introduce some form of National Service?

In a sense, if you have ever been in the Army, you never really leave it, or perhaps it is nearer the mark to say that the Army never completely lets you go. Once a soldier, always a soldier, but, over the years, I have been very bad at keeping up with my army connections... have been often, kindly, chid for it by old friends and past comrades. I am always delighted to encounter them, overjoyed in fact, but it is not in my nature to seek them out, or to relish large formal gatherings. I don't go to Regimental dinners, or attend the annual Hyde Park Cavalry Memorial Parade as I know very well I ought. However, as chance would have it, life coming in lumps as it always does, I was to revisit my old regiment twice in 2006.

An invitation, a command really, that has been long in the diary suddenly came into alarming focus in the summer of that year, we were to attend a parade and garden party in the presence of the Regiment's Colonel in Chief, the King of Jordan. The instructions specified that along with my medals and a bowler hat I was to carry a rolled umbrella. But where was that wretched 'gamp', I hadn't used it in twenty years, not since I was last doing time in the Ministry of Defence?

The house is still full of umbrellas left behind by guests on that happy but wet April day a dozen years back when Louise and Massimo were married. One of them almost looked the part, but when I opened it I found that it had 'Euro' emblems emblazoned on it – how came such a subversive, hated object to survive under this patriotic roof I wondered? I fancied that it might just do, for show.... but if it were to rain on the parade, what unimaginable shame to hoist such a banner, or what idiocy to sit there getting drenched, leaving the beastly thing furled?

As it happened I had a need to go to London about then, so I left early one morning, giving myself time to visit the rubbish dump, a likely find for almost any artefact, then the handiest of the charity shops in Sherborne, on my way to catch the train. No luck, all were drawn blank, every one. But then my fortunes suddenly changed, my vis-à-vis in the train was a neighbour from the village. "Is there by any chance an old gent's umbrella knocking about in the Manor House?" I asked. There was, and I might borrow it.

What luck too that my neighbour had other plans for her journey than to chat. She read her *Daily Telegraph*, I did the work that I had set aside those precious two hours for. We maintained that amicable silence which is only possible between old acquaintances, and which can be so comfortable and valued.

∽❦∾

DO I need to tell you – perhaps you have read before, and remember – how rare and reluctant are my London visits? I dislike the place and it seems to dislike me: time there always drags dreadfully, I don't know what to do with myself or with it.

Lunch was quite fun, at a sheltered pavement table at the Spaghetti House in the Haymarket, rain occasionally pouring down. The weather had at last broken after a late-June heat wave, and the air was heavy. I do love to watch the world go by, it's a taste I gained in Paris as a young man where, of all wonders, the Army once sent me on some course of military instruction. But after lunch, what on earth was I to do until the cocktail hour, when I was due to attend the launch of a friend's book at 127 Piccadilly, the Cavalry and Guards Club?

My feet took me to Burlington House. It was wise of them, that handsome courtyard must be one of the pleasantest places in all London to sit and pass the time on a sultry day. Shaded, uncrowded, quiet, no one asks you for money or enquires what business you have there, and the air is for ever moving. I lost the sense that I usually have of being Septimus Harding – do you remember that chapter in *The Warden* entitled 'A Long Day in London'?

The Summer Exhibition was on, Sir Joshua Reynolds's statue had a garland of flowers, a bandolier about its shoulder, and the Royal Academy courtyard was dominated by a gigantic Damien Hirst bronze entitled 'The Virgin Mother'.

The sculptor had borrowed the pose of the Degas *Ballerina*, but the figure was naked, heavily pregnant, on one side partially flayed so as to show the musculature, and was so enormously tall that the girl's enigmatic and mildly disturbing face could comfortably look into the upper story windows of the Royal Society of Chemists, whose rooms form the east side of the court.

I have no idea what the artistic intention of the piece was, but sitting with its half butchered side out of view, I thought it powerful, touching, beautiful: I was grateful to find a modern work of art that I could relate to, even if I could not understand it, and it was part pastiche anyway. The lady next to me on the bench approved it too, but "Ought to be shot!" was the scandalised comment that I heard another lady mutter as she passed.

The Summer Exhibition itself disappointed, except that it was what I had expected. I walked through all the galleries mentally challenging each room "Arrest me if you can!", but none did. I find myself to be completely out of tune with what modern artists try to do, ditto composers, ditto poets: if they mean to communicate something that is in their heads they entirely fail, with me.

The journey home was as fortunate as was the journey out. An acquaintance boarded the train when it made a seasonal stop at Wimbledon, she was for Axminster, and we chatted happily all the way to Sherborne. When I got home Diana greeted me with the words "They've left you an umbrella, from the Manor, I found it waiting in the back porch... your own umbrella is in the oak chest in the hall!"

There is a moral to this story I feel, which female readers may perhaps be itching to point out – before you go haring off after a wild goose, thinking that you have lost something, consult your wife, she knows where everything is.

∽∘∽

THE mad umbrella hunt had been all wasted effort. I didn't need the wretched thing: for the first time in my life, as I like to think, I was late for parade. We missed it entirely in fact, due to being hopelessly caught up in traffic jams between home and Norfolk. But we made the Garden Party, and achieved one of my objects; I secured an introduction for Diana to His Majesty King Abdullah II. Diana had been at school in Malaya with his mother. Both service children, they had been good friends, and she was curious to revisit the relationship, should this be mutually welcome.

The young King, in build and mien so like his unforgettable, heroic father whom I remembered well from when we were cadets together at Sandhurst, was charming and receptive. He asked for my card, that lacking, took pencil and paper from an aide and wrote Diana's name down – what grace in so important a young man! I later heard another aide passing our details up the line by telephone, so, who knows, something may come of my, I hope uncharacteristic, pushiness?

(It did. Christmas brought a card for Diana from the Royal Palace in Amman.)

∽∘∽

THIS visit to my old regiment had come shortly after one made barely two months before, when, at my own suggestion, I was writing an article for *The Field* to be entitled 'Would I Join the Army Today?'. My intention was to offer some counter-balance to the appalling press coverage my old employer had then been recently receiving. The deaths of recruits at Deepcut Barracks and so on; it was before the war casualties started to flow; the media were biting where they later fawned.

I would never have sought, nor have accepted, the writing commission had I not been certain of my answer to the question in advance. Sure enough, I found my old regiment to be essentially the same as I had left it, but totally different… better, much better really. Thirty years back, when I gave up command, we thought ourselves to be pretty good, but today's army is tested, regularly sharpened, in a way that we only occasionally were. Going back to my old home again had I felt immensely proud, immensely reassured.

You might think that I was wearing rose-tinted spectacles, but, if you learn nothing else in thirty-something years soldiering, you learn to take the measure of an outfit. It doesn't take long – it soon tells you, by the feel of the thing: you are not apt to be fooled. It's like getting onto a strange horse, or, for all I know, picking up someone else's rod or gun, it says to you, or, if you should be out of luck, it doesn't, "I'm the business!".

⋘∽⋙

IT WAS the same second time round, when we went up for King Abdullah's visit. Not long back from Iraq, and with a squadron warned for Afghanistan, they gave us a dinner on a scale and in a style that must I guess be almost unique in today's world, with old regiments being feck-lessly thrown into the melting pot, a shrinking Army for ever wanted here and there, for ever on the move.

There were a hundred and thirty of us dining, and far down the long mess room, in which you could have fitted a cricket pitch and possibly a bowler's run, two rather rowdy tables marked where a cluster of 'my' offi-cers were seated, amongst them were two of my cousins whom I had recruited into our regiment, and who have done me proud.

Pressed to join them at their table I knew better than to do so, I would have been a Banquo at their feast, but I was made happy by their presence and enjoyed their joviality vicariously, at a distance. After dinner a kind friend suggested to me that I should take it as a compliment that so many of that particular cohort attended the reunion: it seemed to me to be just as likely that they got together to yarn about the shared horrors of an old cap-tivity!

My only regret about this happy return to what I privately call 'the crack unit', borrowing a phrase coined by a Barnsley newspaper reporter writing about us years ago, long before the word 'crack' had its present nasty associations, was that I was unable to show Diana round the Officers Mess. The dinner had been of course, except for one uniformed lady, an all-male affair, and the tea party under canvas, out-of-doors.

It's difficult to explain to someone who hasn't seen regimental life from the inside just how important the Mess is. Ideally, it is somewhere to be proud of, a paradigm of excellence and of what a regiment expects of its officers, history put to work, a place from which to go out to do your duty, and a home to return to, duty done. The pictures and silver of four regi-

– 28 –

ments were gathered and lovingly displayed there, amongst them many old friends. I can truly say that I have never seen, nor expect to see a better Mess.

As we sat at dinner it was a special pleasure that the portrait of the old Colonel-in-Chief of the 13th/18th Hussars, Queen Mary, was in view, I remembered it so well from my first evening in the mess half a century before. She seemed to stare across the room in her rather beady, imperious way, at her granddaughter, Princess Margaret, who lately held the same office with the 15th/19th Hussars. The two regiments, conjoined, so sensibly and happily are now called The Light Dragoons. Save your smiles, but I truly believe that it is the best regiment in the whole British Army.

I would particularly have wished to have shown Diana a portrait by Simon Elwes that was my leaving present to my fellow officers. The artist died just as I was giving up command, and the picture for some reason remained unsold with his effects: a large canvas, I bought it at auction for less than it cost to get framed. It is of an officer who had served with us some many years before, in our then full-dress uniform, the subject the bearer of what is to my mind the most enviable title in all the many pages of Debrett. Who wouldn't like to called Lord Huntingfield?

The small plaque on the frame recording my gift, and the unofficial working jersey that the officers and warrant officers still wear, and which I first introduced some three decades before, are the sole marks that I have left upon the regiment that was my home and second family for twenty years: it is more than any individual can expect. The whole point of regimental service is that each one of us is both everything and nothing. As the late CGS General Jackson memorably put it, "The Army is all 'us-us', not 'me-me'".

❧

I JUST dread hearing the news these days. Soldiers must of course go where they are told, and do what they are told when they get there. Nor do they join the army to avoid danger, the best of them join to seek it out. As was written of a founding branch of my old regiment, *"Their's not to reason why..."*, we all know the next line of that poem.

But if serving soldiers may not ask such questions it is surely our duty to do so, in whose name they are deployed and who stay safe at home. Like so many, I allowed myself to be persuaded that the invasion of Iraq was vital to our peace and security here, in these islands: like so many, I have come to think it was a case of political humbug, hubristic thimble-rigging.

The deployment to Afghanistan seems to me both to deny history and to defy reason. I cannot help comparing our politicians' liking for foreign neo-imperialist adventures with their total failure to protect our shores against... yes both if you think of it, *"against infection and the hand of war"*.

WHILST in Norfolk we stayed with cousins whom I seldom these days see but with whom we, my siblings and I, shared much of our childhood and teenage years – they staying here when their father was abroad with his county regiment, we spending some part of our school holidays there when occasion served.

The family home is a magnificent, storied, Tudor manor house of extraordinary interest and beauty, the centre of a farm and shooting estate. The place has for me a halo of childhood memories, not all creditable, as you shall learn, but it was dreamlike to return and explore the old place again.

In the poultry yard, out of devilment or incompetence, I don't remember which, I once shot a chicken with my cousin's airgun. The worst part of the crime was that I and my accomplices hid the corpse, leaving it for foxes in a nearby wood, meat being strictly rationed at the time: I have never been permitted by my cousins to forget it.

Today that poultry yard is lorded over by a herd of peafowl in moult, including two plaintive chicks, survivors of a brood of seven – foxes evidently still being in the offing at Gowthorpe. For souvenirs I carried away a hen's magnificent strong primary, the very image of an old quill pen, and a cock's tail feather, which I keep by me as I write.

The liquid beauty of the rainbow eye in the cock's feather, which seems to breath in the moving air, raises question which science merely begs. If you can believe that such a thing could *evolve* by chance, or by trial and error, you can surely believe anything – Genesis for instance? I give up wondering, in one sense, and just wonder gratefully at the loveliness of the thing.

IV

July 14th – 22nd.

"THE Times or *Guardian* please" Miles said, when I offered to buy him a newspaper. We were waiting at Sherborne station for the train that would shortly whisk him and Othello off on the first stage of their long journey back to Japan. "It will have to be *The Times*" I replied, having never in my life bought a copy of *The Guardian* (guardian indeed, and promoter, of so many of the daft ideas that have tended to geld and denature the country that I love).

Miles and I understand each other pretty well, and both smile. It's a leg-pull really, suggesting the different worlds we live in. It was bad enough having to put money into the pocket of an anti-monarchist, whose paper I read eagerly when I do not have to pay for it but will not have in the house... but to be seen on Sherborne station purchasing a copy of *The Guardian!*

Neither Othello nor I are great conversationalists, and I really had to put my mind to it to engage him in anything like easy chat as we sat together on the platform bench. What had he enjoyed most in his short stay with us, I asked? It was a lucky stroke. He reeled off, numbering them in merit order, "The tractor ride, the polo match, apple cricket, shooting penalties on the lawn, pick-a-back polo, playing chess, the bonfire....", jumping at last to ".... 100, climbing all those stairs". He had slept in his father's childhood attic bedroom, the one with the cyclopean eye.

It was a list that raises more questions than you will want answered. Suffice it to say that for a halcyon few days, and for the first time in ten years, we had all our four 'children' staying with us, and they brought all their children. With the blessed inclusion of one nanny, we slept fourteen in the house.

In preparation I had set out croquet on the lawn. The hoops, pin, mallets and balls were all instantly seized on and misapplied by our swarming grandchildren who had their own ideas of what games they were to play. The World Cup had just finished, Test Matches were in the air: goalposts and a wicket were wanted (I should have thought of that). A pair of pitchforks and a length of binder-twine soon met the one need, and the orchard path, and the young apples, discarded by trees too parched to support them, the other.

And **my** best memory? After the children's bedtime on the last evening, before our house party broke up, over supper in the kitchen hearing our four young swapping memories of shared school holidays. Remembering the time when, in their early teens, my two boys suddenly found that they had two sisters, off-the-peg as it were, and the girls two brothers. We have been from the start a very, very happy family, and I... a very lucky man.

I HAVE described it as a halcyon time, those few days with our family, because, except for during a couple of tactfully timed and welcome bursts of rain, we had all been able to live, play and, to Diana's great relief, eat out-of-doors under truly kingfisher skies. England, we were told, had never known such temperatures. Perhaps by the time you read this we shall have had another such July, but it doesn't seem likely (we didn't, July '07 was to be the wettest on record!).

Thunder was for ever forecast, but it never reached us... except in the news headlines. The Levant blew up, and, again, I wonder as I write how that tragedy will look this time next year (no better, worse if anything). Are we, as I suspect, on the threshold of something not far off world war: or will it have blown over, with just uncounted graves and enduring local misery to show for it?

In church on the Sunday, after our visitors had all gone, the first lesson, a rather bloody passage, from the Old Testament of course, reminded me of how often perverted religion is at the bottom of our troubles. It was a comfort to reflect that ours is not by nature a fanatical country, we church-goers take what we need from our religion, the gentle side of it, and let the rest go. Is it something to do with a temperate climate, and a sense of humour: let's hope we are not losing either?

∽∽∾

IT has been a season of extraordinary growth hereabouts, just the right amount of rainfall, generous sun, the wisteria that my parents planted on two sides of the house more rapidly aggressive than I can remember. You could almost see it growing, with its strong instinct for getting into wher-ever it is not wanted, especially into guttering and under roof tiles.

For the first time ever wood pigeons nested in its generous corsage, under our bedroom window, the cock bird usually pausing on the open sill to give two-and-a-bit stanzas of his familiar song before descending to feed his chicks – since he kept rather early hours this might be at five o'clock in the morning.

We all no doubt put our own words to the ring dove's music, I borrow my mother's – "It's too true Gertrude, it's to true Gertrude, it's...": I think of him as a feathered Bishop Proudie, trying to placate his tyrant of a wife, and always cut off in mid-sentence by a dismissive frown.

How and when the squabs got away from the nest I never exactly knew, suddenly the parents' comings and goings ceased. They were running busy relays to the nest one day, then the next day nothing. Diana reported seeing Toffee, the gamekeeper's ginger tom, hanging around the lawn like a corner boy one evening: that was the only clue, but there were no feath-ers to suggest that he bagged one.

Birds so often mark a special time, claiming a share in the memory. One morning, whilst I was sitting on the front doorstep, before the children and the house were quite awake, a robin, flying down from that wisteria, for a tiny fraction of a passing second, but gilding a moment never to be forgotten, no doubt mistaking me for a piece of garden furniture, perched on my shoulder on its way to hunt for insects on the lawn.

July 30th.

HOW shamefully often one's credulity leads one into needless scrapes. It has happened to me twice in recent days. The first occasion was in the comparative privacy of the vegetable garden, where I have been propagating strawberry plants, layering the young suckers by pinning them down with wire staples into small pots sunk level with the soil. Watering them assiduously, congratulating myself on how they prospered, each one to be the saving of 50p next spring, telling anybody who would listen what a clever and thrifty husbandman and gardener I was.

It was only when I had lifted the first two dozen, snipping their umbilical cords, shifting them in triumph to the shelter of the potting shed, that I focussed sufficiently sharply on them to realize that at least a quarter, the most prized, willing and prolific, were not strawberry plants at all but fine young specimens of *Rununculus repens*, my old enemy Creeping Buttercup, or 'the tick' as I call it as I painstaking lever it out of every corner of the vegetable patch.

Then, worse, in church, my critical eye lighted on, as I thought, the wrong, quite ridiculous, dates given for the great Samuel Johnson in the new hymn books we have recently adopted, they would have it that he had lived from 1822 to 1882. "How dim can you get" I asked myself, "placing the giant of his age in the 19th century?".

I don't like the new hymnal's name "Common Praise". Those ninnies in the hierarchy that decide such things have evidently not noticed that the word 'common' has acquired an unfortunate meaning since Cranmer's day, but I approve their taste, at least in the inclusion of "City of God, how broad and far…", with its splendid final verse, so typically Johnsonian, so lapidary, I have always thought – "In vain the surge's angry shock, in vain the shifting sands…": it is not in *Hymns Ancient and Modern*.

I muttered my complaint to the Church Warden as I left, explaining why I was temporarily purloining a copy of the offending book: she was impressed, wide-eyed almost at my omniscience, grateful, mildly apologetic on behalf of the 'management'. That evening I wrote a letter of remonstrance to the publishers, copying it by e-mail to the Rector, and corrected the dates in the hymnal that I had brought home.

But, in the waking hours next morning, when so many of my less idiotic thoughts present themselves uninvited, the knots of the previous evening suddenly of themselves miraculously untied – on this occasion to music, as Bishop Proudie announced breakfast to his chicks – I suddenly remembered being once told that, just as there were two Samuel Butlers, there was a second, later, lesser, Samuel Johnson, an American non-conformist divine.

I retrieved my letter before Brett our faitful postie could collect it, checked my facts in the Library, ate humble pie by e-mail to the rector. I didn't think it necessary to say anything to the Church Warden: with luck she will go on thinking that I am wiser than I am: no one else need know.

August 1st.

IT'S official, it was 'the hottest July on record', and it ended with the weather at last breaking yesterday. When I rode Dandy over Dungeon in a bracing wind tall clouds were racing each other across a sky that in previous weeks had seemed almost to have emptied itself for ever.

The horses will be grateful; despite their distant Arab extraction, they don't seem to like intense heat. I would work one of them each morning before insect-life and the grandchildren were about: but visited later in the day they always had a domino of flies covering their poor faces. How uncomfortable that sight always makes one feel, whether it be a African waif on TV, or one of your own dear horses.

It was lucky the weather held for as long as it did. Friday saw us at Broadlands for the Game Fair, and on Sunday we were at the Cartier International Day on Smith's Lawn, to watch England beat New Zealand at polo. There were enormous crowds at both events, but as different crowds as you could possibly imagine, the one all casually doggy, the other self-consciously *chic*.... not to say 'chick'.

Cartier is such a treat for us country mice, we go up every year wide-eyed, wondering who and what we shall see, our parking badge, with delightful irony, describing us as being VVIPs! In fact of course I am 'singing for my supper', I go there to work, but they treat us royally, and we really enjoy it.

I have become used to the eager then suddenly blank faces of the paparazzi when we arrive in the reception area, swiftly lowering their cameras as they recognize us as nonentities. We are used also to drawing the full length of the glittering metropolitan 'covert', up- then down-wind, across and through, Bellini in hand (how I love that drink!), without finding a single person present whom we know.

Usually we are herded along with the also-ran demi-mondaines, our table in some far corner of the marquee, but this time "Wow!", we were sharing Jilly Cooper's table, seated not two paces away from our host – fame at last? I have a very slight acquaintance with that celebrated lady, but as she was three places down from me I didn't feel inclined to exploit it, and was later duly chid by Diana for my timidity. I prefer comfort to celebrity any day, am socially unadventurous, no lion-hunter, as you may perhaps have detected, and the charming young ladies on my either side were quite company enough for me.

On both our outings, to Broadlands and to Windsor, the competing traffic was horrendous. As we inched our way from Smith's Lawn on the Sunday evening Classic FM was playing Beethoven's Ninth Symphony – for a wonder the whole thing, all four movements, not just a tantalising excerpt – I couldn't believe it. I fancy that I can remember every note of the base line in the final, choral, section, and sang-along quietly all the way until the peaceful-tempestuous finale, when, as luck would have it, the traffic eased.

ONE of the great pleasures of riding in the middle of nowhere, entirely on your own, is that you can sing out loud, as loud as you like in fact, without causing anyone annoyance or alarm; I often do it. When I am riding down Dungeon, as I was today, I am always looking for a particularly precious spanner that I lost up there eighteen months ago, consciously retracing the steps Dandy and I took on the morning when we re-hung the gate on the hill, which had somehow come off its hinge.

It had been a rather sheepish route. Having fixed the gate and re-mounted, I had become suddenly aware from their hoof beats that its owner's point-to-pointers were doing some fast work just out of sight but in the same field. With the sound, in the same moment, came the guilty thought that, on the principle of "What the eye doesn't see...", I hadn't, as I ought to have done, sought permission of its owner to tamper with his gate.

I had sunk the hill quickly, keeping in dead ground, and nipped off at a canter, trusting to get through the far gate and away before they should know of my presence. Just short of the gate I realized that the spanner had dropped from its hastily knotted mooring at the saddle-D, and that I couldn't then return to look for it. I have been hoping to stumble on it ever since.

As I searched the ground for the umpteenth time this morning I sang the first song that really caught on with me in my nursery days. It's a girl's song, our nanny used to sing it, but I adjust the words to the occasion.

"Some day my prince will come..."

August 3rd.

THE beans are getting pursy, there are apples lying around everywhere in the orchard – far more numerous than just the odd 'cricket ball' of a fortnight back – some of them enormous, with the beginning of a smile on their faces, looking quite potable if not edible, and you can already find black blackberries in the hedge. Everything seems to be going over... Help! We don't want autumn yet.

Yet half of me is always secretly hurrying the bean plants, the straggling courgette vines and the sweet peas, especially the sweet peas, onto the compost heap. How I hate cutting sweet peas, it's such a mimsy job, snip, snip, snip: no job for a man at all, let alone a soldier. And I hate digging potatoes too, always swear that I will never grow them again, but somehow always do.

It's love/hate really, love always winning, I'm seldom happier that in the vegetable garden. But I do like it to be tidy, and I was born impatient; these I know are not the characteristics of a proper gardener. "You should see how other people let their roses grow all higgledy-piggledy" Diana says to me, as I set about trimming back the Banksia in the kitchen yard. "*They* never did regimental duty" I explain: "I know, that's just the problem" comes her long-suffering reply.

It's an eternal argument, but the roses are at least one department of our garden which actually seems to flourish under strict military discipline. For instance, although I always 'prune' the Banksia with an electric hedge-trimmer it was better than ever this year, simply covered with tiny yellow blossoms. For once I am allowed to carry my point.

∽◯◯∼

THE *Spectator* recently carried an article by Paul Johnson, in which he tried to answer a question put to him by his teenage grand-daughter: "What was the most exciting moment in your life?" The reply he gave was that it was when, as a twelve-year-old, he had his first view out over a magnificent vista in the Lake District. When I had read the article I found that it cost me a night's sleep trying to answer the same question for myself.

My first thoughts were of some of the rides I have had here-and-there on borrowed horses. There was mare called Colette that the Border Hunt found for me on my first visit to their dreamland country; Mr Christian, the Aintree horse, a true gentleman with a snaffle in his mouth, with the Eggesford; Pikey, the delightfully named gipsy pinto – you are not supposed to use that word 'pikey' these days in case you hurt some gipsy's tender feelings... there, I've done it twice, please visit me in prison – with the Axe Vale; and of course the never-to-be-forgotten Softy with the Cattistock at the end of last season.

And there was the great-hearted government charger, a Hanoverian giant mysteriously called Farouk, that I had at my disposal when I was adjutant of my regiment in Germany. I am sure he would have jumped a house, cold, if I had had the nerve to ask him: we had a lot of fun together. I used to ride him on parade, in full fig, with the band playing and all. Do line cavalry adjutants still ride on parade? Soldiering is surely a bit too serious these days for that sort of frill: my old regiment has lost its splendid band I know.

However, horses, much though I love them, somehow do not quite fill the bill. Music seems nearer the mark, singing for the great Dr Douglas Fox, that one-armed paladin, at Clifton – to some extent he has 'conducted' my life ever since, I admired his courage and his character so much, and often think of him.

Perhaps singing the *Dona Nobis Pacem* that closes Bach's B Minor Mass in Bristol Cathedral was my most exciting moment: Douglas Fox said that hearing the increasing majesty of that chorus was like threading Cheddar Gorge. Or perhaps it should be the finale of the Choral Symphony, no school had I believe ever attempted that musical 'north face' before we scaled it. *Tochter aus Elysium* … indeed, who cares that the ridiculous 'Europe' has pinched that sacred banner?

∽∝∾

FINDING things can bring unforgettable pleasure and excitement. There was the knapped flint that I turned up in a flowerbed, and which I keep by me as a talisman, connecting today, this very minute as I touch it, with that moment two or three thousand years ago when some stone age man dropped it here, on our ground.

And there was the royal family tree that I found amongst papers in the attic. Painstakingly engrossed on parchment at the time of the Restoration, it records the descent of the crown from William the Conqueror to Charles II, with countless royal collaterals, their places of birth and burial. Itself restored, it hangs, a daily wonder, on our back staircase.

∽∝∾

THESE were indeed all great excitements, but did they quite measure up as the memory of a lifetime? Perhaps more to the point was standing opposite the west door of Westminster Abbey on a wintry June day half a century ago, rooted to the ground of course, 'eyes front' much of the time, but with perhaps as good a view of the Coronation as had anybody in the whole wide watching world that memorable day. I was a cadet in my first term at Sandhurst; we were lining the processional route.

I saw my cousin the admiral arrive, dismount, then afterwards remount and ride away again. His position at Court required him to ride as escort on a grey horse immediately behind or before the state coach. A year later I was to command a church parade at Sandhurst for that same cousin. That's something to remember, briefly commanding the whole Sandhurst entry in front of that fine Regency palace of a building, a thousand men and more attendant and dependent on your word, on your remembering the whole grand rigmarole, unprompted, and getting it exactly right.

It was a treat that the Academy Adjutant had conditionally promised me. Seated next to him at a formal dinner night in my first, hectic, junior term, he had said "If you get to be a Senior Under Officer in your final term we'll invite your cousin, the C-in-C Home Fleet, over from Portsmouth to take the salute one Sunday, and you can command the parade". I did: they did: he did: I did.

It was typical of that splendid man then Major, later Lieutenant General, Vernon Erskine Crum to be so kind and so particular with an awkward, shy young man. No doubt heading for the top, he died tragically young. My last memory of him is of his suddenly falling into step beside me on Whitehall's pavement one lunch hour, when I was doing penal servitude in the Ministry of Defence.

He greeted me, a young major then, as if we had seen each other every day in the intervening decade, asked me how and what I did, made some typically dry and kindly response to my no doubt lame reply. I felt ten feet tall, to know that that great man still had an approving eye on me.

I can picture him now, his back view in Scots Guards uniform, on his grey charger, leading us up the steps of the Old Building at Sandhurst on the day Intake XII passed out. What a *gentleman*, what *grace* – if I overuse those two words, please forgive me.

THE sequel of the Sandhurst Church Parade was that my childless distant cousin took me up, befriended me, and made me his heir. "There'll be no money" he said, "but you will have all my naval and family bits and pieces". When he died I was that young major, just described, in my first staff appointment sitting, bored witless and in a muddle you may be sure, at my Whitehall desk, 'planning World War III', when the First Lord's office suddenly rang…. which must have made me sit up.

I was to present myself at Portsmouth next day for my cousin's Memorial Service. As I climbed the gangway to board the frigate that took his ashes to be strewn off The Nab, the First Lord, a full admiral, stood there, saluting me… me! It was a lesson in how a great service looks after its own, to the end.

He had *"done the State some service"*, that warrior cousin of mine. He belonged to the generation that fought in both World Wars, and which saw a great deal more excitement during its lifetime than most of us do. Born in 1891, he went to sea, after schooling at Osborne, in 1908, and, along with our Queen's father, was at the Battle of Jutland.

I can only guess what the most exciting moment in his life was, but surely somewhere high on the list must have been that morning in March 1941 when "searching the horizon on the starboard bow with his glasses, he calmly reported that he saw two large cruisers with a smaller one ahead of them crossing the bows of the battle fleet from starboard to port". Minutes later the cream of the Italian fleet was on the bottom.

That was the opening of the Battle of Matapan. John Edelsten had just joined Admiral Cunningham, whose memoirs I quote from, as his Chief-of-Staff, and found himself at a hinge in history. (Don't you love that word *calmly* in Lord Cunningham account?). This house is full of reminders of my cousin's naval and Court service. When I was recently scrabbling around in the dusty tallet where we keep such things, looking for a seedbox for my strawberry plants, there were all his much travelled and be-labelled sea chests and trunks. I keep my cousin's picture in my dressing room, close by my father's: he was very good to me, I never forget him.

❧

YOU are watched and judged the whole time at Sandhurst, and you get your palm read. When I was later sent by my regiment to serve on the staff there, I learnt that it was not by chance that that great man the Academy Adjutant had been seated next to me at the dinner table, he was giving me the once-over. It was lucky that I didn't know; naivety is a vital part of a young man's armoury.

Another, more prophetic and intelligible, straw in the wind had my history tutor tell me that I was probably not ruthless enough to get to the top of the army, but had a facility for writing that might come in one day, and which I should cultivate. It was a fine, memorable and, yes, exciting thing to command my regiment, to manoeuvre 45 tanks, and especially to have a full stable and a band at my disposal, but I was never near gaining the front rank of my profession.

Was the first time I saw an article that I had written appear in print, or the moment when I held in my hand a copy of my first book, the most exciting of my life? Possibly so... but perhaps the moment is yet to come.

❧

MORNING and evening, most days, I climb up to this attic to ask my computer – how I wish it were a horse, I would understand it so much better – if it has any messages for me, and it throws up on the screen the usual unequal mix of chaff and grain. One day last spring, just after Dandy had stopped jumping and I was in the dumps, a message from *Horse & Hound* came up. Would I interview the Prince of Wales as part of a series they were running? Imagine it, he had asked for me, by name, actually conditioned that I, and nobody else, should do the job!

Clarence House a few weeks later was terrifying, until I was actually in the presence of that truly charming prince. "Don't mention hunting" his staff had cautioned me: his first question to me was "How's hunting going...?". That May morning must surely be somewhere up the list of my most exciting moments... but there, I have barely mentioned home, or family.

That same computer brought me a quite different sort of message a few weeks later reminding me how very much thicker blood is than water, and bringing suddenly alive the invisible wiring that connects us with our immediate kin. I give you the exchange of messages, mine first, then the answer that so much disturbed me, they explain themselves....

I had sent.... *"Miles, Happy birthday, where ever you are; thinking of you. Your fortieth year, gosh, I remember the moment you were born! Love from us both, D&D."*.... back came... *"Daddy, Thanks for remembering my birthday. Hope this doesn't worry you too much since the war is over now, but actually I've been spending the day on the road from Damascus to Beirut - a beautiful trip on fantastic roads strangely enough. I'm over here for 2-and-a-half weeks to give our regular Muslim war journalists a break - should be filming UN peacekeepers arriving mostly. Miles"*

I had supposed, in sending my younger son, who is a busy and successful TV journalist, 39th birthday greetings, that he was still where he last called me from, which was in North Korea. To find him at the seat-of-war, albeit during a ceasefire which I didn't for a moment trust, was like a sudden blow under the ribs. It was some days before I knew him to be safe back in Tokyo. Two TV journalists were kidnapped and one was shot, whilst he was in the Lebanon.

On reflection, I think 'giving away' my younger stepdaughter, Louise, at her wedding, in our church here, is one of the most memorable days of my life. I can never forget walking her up the path through the orchard that April afternoon, meeting my old friend the Rector in his billowing robes at the church door, and then, as we followed him up the aisle, the whole congregation turning to look with wonder at the beautiful girl on my arm.

Perhaps happiness is more to be looked for and treasured than excitement; I can't remember a happier day in this happiest of places than that of Louise's wedding.

ONE excitement that I never looked for came quite out of nowhere. My niece, who after serving with the war dogs in Iraq next found herself posted as vet to the Kings Troop Royal Horse Artillery, possibly... no certainly, the best job in her line of work in the whole army, asked us up as guests of the Troop, for the State Opening of Parliament.

It was thrilling enough to be in a horsed barracks, to hear and watch all the military bustle, to feel the excitement, but, suddenly, the Honorary Colonel of the Troop, an old acquaintance turned to me. "Got your hat?" he asked, "Stand there...!" indicating a spot in front of the small crowd of friends and relatives who were gathered by the barracks gate to see the guns depart. Imagine it, I was to take the salute as the guns left for their march across London to St James's Park.

We followed them, in a bus, saw them go though their drills, fire the salute in the Park, arriving and departing full tilt, limbering and unlimbering. After that we were admitted, just a few dozen of us, to the fore-court at the Palace to watch, almost at touching distance, as the royal procession returned, the Sovereign's Escort, two hundred horses or so, massing before us in the confined, railed space. Then it was back to St John's Wood, to take the salute, meet all those proudly turned eyes again, as the guns returned.

Dining-out on it back in Dorset, and you may be sure that I told the story endlessly to anybody who would listen to me, no doubt in some cases more than once. I also had to tell them that the only hitch in proceedings was that, no doubt due to my chest swelling with pride, mid-morning, whilst trapesing through the Park to the Palace, my braces snapped. I had surreptitiously to hold my trousers up with one hand whilst acknowledging the salutes of the returning gun crews. As a rule I never quit the house without a knife, a hoof-pick and a hank of binder-twine about me somewhere in my pockets, but for some reason I didn't seem to have any string with my London clothes – it's a lesson.

Perhaps the story leaves you cold, or at least leaves you smiling piti-fully. Have I conveyed to you how much it meant, suddenly, under the amazed eyes of so many of my family, to be promoted to such a unique honour as receiving the salute of the King's Troop RHA, guns and all? As I say, once a soldier always a soldier: it's a thought that gives some meaning to another long remembered snatch from an old song, familiar from my childhood....

"Old soldiers never die, they only fade away".

V

August 8th.

"ARE you riding this morning?" Diana asked in surprise: both the horses went out yesterday, and we had a full day ahead. I nodded not venturing my reason, which was to pick up the litter that I had noticed on my beat when we had ridden it together; she doesn't find my constantly hopping off to retrieve trash amusing, so I save it for another day. Also, driving back together from Dorchester in the afternoon I had seen that some genius had deposited an enormous white plastic container on the grass bank, just outside the village. Had I been alone I would have stopped to remove it: I wanted to check this morning to see if it was still there.

I took Bella, to avoid the palaver of bringing both horses into the stable, saddled her in the gateway, and, giving myself a slightly naughty treat, set out across my neighbour's meadows, Lady Mead and Brook Furlong, headed for his wood.

I call it 'slightly naughty' because, although he very kindly permits me to ride there, I tend to avail myself of the permission when he is away. I can't imagine that it actually pleases him to see me on his land; in his place it wouldn't please me. So I do it rarely, and as covertly as possible if, as now, he is at home.

Using fieldcraft learnt at Sandhurst we drop, Bella and I, into a hollow that traverses what was once, before I knew it, two, but is now just one meadow, make Great Wootton Wood unobserved, and ride up through that heavenly place onto the shoulder of Dungeon Hill, dismounting when we reach the road where my work starts.

The gateway onto Park Lane, the start of my 'beat', is a favourite stopping place for the *litterati*. As noticed yesterday, there are the remains of a picnic and shopping expedition lying there, the packaging of a glue-tube, a sandwich box, plastic bottle, and, because the *litterati* are such *nice* people, with such genteel manners, paper napkins.

Leading Bella at the length of her reins – unlike Dandy, she doesn't chew them – I set out to trudge the mile or so home, picking up as I go, she snatching bites out of the verge as opportunity offers. Bella at least approves my mad obsession, but I have to watch her, she is a great nudger, and is very impatient. At one moment, when I am bent over, reaching at full stretch into the depths of a bramble bush, she gives me such a push with her nose as all but had me topple head-over-heels into the middle of it.

Soon we are nearly home, and I have a complete carrier bag full, and it's not three days' worth. What's the point of acting nursemaid to feckless trash, with the rest of the world indifferent, I ask myself. Should I give up? Never!

THAT stuff I wrote in my Cattistock hunt report about not being able to see too clearly what was going on beyond my horse's ears was not entirely a journalist's exaggeration. I used to have wonderfully sharp long sight, could just about name any common bird by its jizz, at any distance. Now things are a bit of a blur, and, at this colourful time of year, if you are looking for roadside litter nature tends to play tricks on you.

For a start, there are all the feathers that the now silent birds drop in their moult, and which often briefly take on the look of human rubbish. There are wan leaves discarded by parched trees that can look like scraps of paper, brilliant golden straws that for a moment pretend to be sweet-wrappings, and gaudy delicious-looking lollipops that turn out to be Wild Arum, Lords-and- ladies, with their poisonous, scarlet berries. They drive me to my books when I get home – more of that in a minute.

Eventually we get to that plastic horror, still crowning the roadside bank. It turns out to be an empty 25 litre, five-gallon to you and me, udderwash container. I acquit the farmer from whose trailer it must have dropped of having meant to leave it there, preferring to blame whoever put it up out of the road onto the bank. I do what he or she should have done, take it along with me, dropping it surreptitiously in a builder's skip in the outskirts of the village.

AS I SAID, those Lords-and-ladies drove me to my books, first to my plant dictionary to get their Latin name, *Arum Maculatum*, from their spotty leaves no doubt, then to one of the loveliest books I have, 'The Children's Book of Wild Flowers & the Story of their Names' by Gareth Browning, illustrated by M.C.Pollard. My copy is inscribed in faultless copperplate to my first mother-in-law, a lady whom I am still much attached to, it is dated 1928.

It tells me that the Wild Arum is also called, Adam and Eve, Ladies-and-gentlemen, Parson-in-the-pulpit, Lamb-in-the-pulpit, Schoolmaster, Adders's-meat, Toad's-meat, Snake's-food, Snake's-meat, Dead-man's-fingers, Lords'-and-ladies'-fingers, Ladies'-fingers, Friar's-cowl, Priest's-hood, Jack-in-the-box, Babe-in-the-cradle, Cuckoo-pint, Cuckoo-babies, Cuckoo-flower, Starch-root, and Starch-wort.

"Long ago" I learn, *"the Wild arum was made to serve a useful household purpose. That was in the days when the fine ladies and gentlemen who went to Court wore stiff and elaborate ruffs around their necks. The use of starch was not common then, and, when it was discovered that the root of the Arum contained a lot of starchy matter, it was employed in stiffening ruffs and other linen".*

What the book doesn't of course say, or even hint at, it being for children, and written in more reticent times, is what Shakespeare all but spells out, writing of another wild flower, when Hamlet's mother describes poor mad Ophelia's end....

"There is a willow grows aslant a brook,
That shows his hoar leaves in the glassy stream;
There with fantastic garlands did she come,
Of crow-flowers, nettles, daisies, and long purples,
That liberal shepherds give a grosser name,
But our cold maids do dead men's fingers call".

I think that calling Wild Arum 'Adam and Eve' is fairly close to what those naughty liberal shepherds were getting at.

THE rams have been almost trouble-free, a real pleasure to have about the place this year. Unlike last summer, when a blind ram, that I called Blunkett, that name being much in the news then, gave us a lot of heartache, and a very old one called Eyore nearly died on us. So far there have been only two dramas.

I left them a day too long in our small paddock, and Mr Yellow (from his ear tag – how I hate those barbaric bureaucratic things), who is a loner, battered his way through a fence onto my neighbour, Mrs Ross's lawn, where I found him looking self-conscious and a bit worried. I caught him with my crook, looped a rope round his neck, and propelled him reluctantly up the drive and through the gate of the big paddock by main force.

Then, that evening, another neighbour's terrier had a go at them, almost hunting one of the rams down, when Diana fortunately arrived and restored order. It could have been a disaster, but in fact acted as an immunisation. I don't think we are likely to have that problem again this summer; it wasn't just the rams that got a fright.

After the incident with the terrier all five of the rams huddled, demoralised and breathless, at the far bottom end of the paddock. It seemed the right thing to do to go and spend time with them, to make sure that they were not permanently injured, just distressed. It was rather remarkable, and something that I have never sensed or noticed before, that, palpably, they drew comfort from my presence.

As their breathing eased – it was one of the hottest of hot days in the hottest July anyone can remember – I edged away from the paddock corner, and, following me, they started at last to graze and settle. Within an hour they made their way cautiously to the trough, and, seeing them drink, I felt able to leave them. It took them a day or so to get the confidence to graze the whole width of the paddock, and to learn to ignore the barking of my neighbour's dogs, which are now, like poor Clarence, *"close mewed up"*.

You've met Mr Yellow; the companions whose company he distains are Messrs Blue 1, Blue 2, Green and Spotty, that last-named having been lucky enough to escape tagging. Unlike some rams we have had in the past, they are a gentle crew, one and all: a happy memory of when the children were with us was of going hand-in-hand with my two small step-granddaughters, Sophia and Marina, to talk to the rams and make a fuss of them.

But one evening, as I walked down the drive with the 'paper there were ructions. Neil had just dropped off a sixth ram, and there was a lot of rather rough sorting out of the pecking-order going on; the new-boy was being given a hard time.

Mr W (short for Woolworths) was soon either driven out of the flock, or elected to keep his own company, for he is always to be found completely on his own. I think he is a youngster, and I guess bottle-reared, for he bleats at me whenever I walk by him, and comes to have his woolly face scratched. Mr W is an absolute dear.

⤬∽∾⤬

"It was a bright summer afternoon, when the harvest was at its height,
and joyful cheers rang ever and anon on the surrounding landscape,
denoting that now another and another farmer's fears were
over, by the last of his corn getting cut..."

WE were at that time of year when towering loads of baled straw were to be seen on all roads heading west; what they do with all those vast quantities of the stuff down there I have never understood. They are always driven with panache, we were nearly plastered against a wall by two mammoth lorries, trailers and all, powering round Marston Magna's curves one morning.

The journey to Castle Cary was getting to be familiar, Melanie had quit London and taken a house there: her stepfather consequently is much in demand as odd-job-man, to make the garden dog-proof, hang pictures and so on.

There is nothing to beat female insouciance and the artistic temperament when it comes to finding a secure purchase on doubtful old walls. Women call screws 'nails', wave their arms vaguely at the site of the miracle you are required to perform, and gabble on about the next two or three jobs that need your undivided attention before you have got your head properly around the one in hand.

"Here they are, I've found them!" Mel cries triumphantly waving a bag of essential metal Ikea gadgets that had blessedly gone missing, "you can do the kitchen shelves now. It's easy, look, here are the instructions". "I don't wish to be told how easy it is" I tell her sternly, "just tell me how clever I am when I have done it".

Have you ever tried to assemble Ikea? It's a form of mental torture garnished with humbug. The instructions, in eighteen languages, kick off with a warning "The assembly should be carried out by a qualified person

… wrong assembly can lead to …. personal injury or damage", but the accompanying picture shows a young girl doing the job.

What of course the instructions don't and can't help you with is hanging the finished article, six heavy shelves, level, un-supported, clear of the ground, on a two-hundred-year-old cottage wall.

You have had enough of this no doubt. The men will have understood what was involved in getting eight two-inch plugs into that wall, placed to the millimetre to meet the Ikea screw-holes: the ladies won't want to know, but will no doubt be quite nice about it, as my wife and her daughter were, but scarcely drawing breath before directing me to the next job.

August 14th.

WE have been under a northerly breeze, at times quite strong, almost continuously for the best part of a fortnight now, with just the odd spot of rain; never more than that. Everywhere is parched, like Melba toast, yuk! Great cracks are opening up in the ground: grass is becoming scarce, except where you don't want it, and the bonfire is getting enormous waiting for the wind to shift into a more neighbour-friendly quarter.

Riding Dandy down off Dungeon this morning, on the baked ground he was more than ever like someone's great grandmother coming down steep stairs. We've decided on a course of action. We are going to have his feet x-rayed when we get home from our impending travels. If we are lucky, and we find that the problem is not deterioration of the bones of his feet, it could be his back that is troubling him, that's fixable. Anyway, the die is cast, we know the next move, which is a help.

Half way down the slope, as ever scanning the ground for my lost spanner, a strange object caught my eye, and caused Dandy at the same time to start. It looked like a giant lemon, but was somehow too garish and not quite solid enough: anyway, what would a lemon of any size be doing on Dungeon Hill?

I couldn't leave it there to mock and puzzle me week-in-week out, so there was nothing for it but to get off. I found that it was an almost deflated lime-green balloon, with streamers attached, fruit of the breeze that I was telling you about. It had a shrunken legend on it – "NEW CAT-ALOGUE OUT NOW: ARGOS".

15th-16th August.

STUBBLE! The best time of the year for riding, just those few days between the visits of the combine and the plough when you can go more-or-less where you like on horseback: how I enjoy it! The wheat fields by Hay Wood, where I noted all that ryegrass in June, had been taken.

Bella and I romped diagonally across the belly of the first field, where the bridle path goes, but where you would never think of riding when a crop is in the ground. Then you must pick your way round the meagre headland, or follow a 'tramline' once the crop has been sprayed: that way I justify myself in taking slight liberties, like riding homeward off the bridle path through the wood, where I delight, but have no right, to go.

The second field hadn't seen the baler yet, or hadn't been 'led', to use a phrase employed by Surtees, which conjures a wonderful picture of straining shire horses carting the crop off to the stackyard. The straw lay waiting to be picked up, in ranks, likes waves before an inshore breeze on a golden sea. Spring must I suppose be the loveliest time of year, but the harvest's aftermath has its beauties.

Riding home across Stonylongs the white hart on the church weather vane confirmed what my bare forearms had already told me, the wind had at last quit the northern quarter and gone round to the west. By lunch time it was steady from the south. I put a match to the bonfire: it went off most satisfyingly, like a rocket.

August 21st.

WEDDINGS seem to go on all night these days, if you see what I mean, and they cost what you used to be able to buy a small house for. I was looking back on a typically sociable Dorset weekend. A barn dance, a polo match and a christening fell to our lot, not to mention the village being in the grip of 'Iron Man' for most of Sunday. And we had Charlie my eldest son staying, with his Anna, and 10½ month-old Stephanie Isobel, my bewitching granddaughter.

It had seemed a good move to get both horses out on the Saturday morning, and, as Diana and I were riding back across my neighbour's meadow towards the church and home, the Captain of Bells was to be seen making his way across the graveyard to the south door. I smelt a rat, or rather smelt orange blossom: there must be a wedding in the offing, and no one had asked us about using our ground for parking.

Sure enough, when I could get to the telephone the Rector confirmed it, full of apologies – not **his** fault. Nor was it anybody's fault as I later found out, they had made other arrangements – but he threw in, no doubt to mollify me, that the bride had been out with hounds that morning.

I went to shut the horses out of the bit of pasture that we use as a parking area, and put up the usual signs. I was pensive; the Rector had made me think about hunting, reminded me how, with the end of the early harvest, a new season would soon be starting.

A FEW years ago an old regimental friend started a polo club in the Blackmore Vale, at West Orchard, beyond Sturminster Newton. Duty and inclination take me there when I can find the time, which is seldom more than on a couple of afternoons a season. On this occasion, as I left to go there, the village was full of wedding traffic, smiling strangers, vaguely lost, all up for a party but not quite sure how to get there.

At West Orchard they were due to play for the Shrimps Cup, so called because it is the smallest silver trophy that you ever saw, about the size of an eggcup. But it has a history, and the late Lord Mountbatten's name engraved on it... and it wasn't cheap, at least not cheap in my money; I had presented it to the club.

The first match was delayed, ponies stuck in traffic, so I went to chat in a presidential sort of way to one of the waiting teams, the way one must, although it doesn't come easily. The team contained two local MFH's; were his hounds really out that morning I asked one of them? Yes, but it was just hound exercise, he told me; he knew all about our village bride. Would I be hunting this season, he parried? "I suppose so", I answered.

Being president of a polo club is something and nothing. It's quite nice to see your name all grandly printed in the Hurlingham Polo Association Year Book, and on the club Fixture Card, but in fact, at least in my case, it involves nothing more that turning up now and then wearing a tie, and occasionally putting your hand in your pocket, or signing a cheque. To mix metaphors, Dick wanted a cat's paw for a figurehead, and, in his old CO, he has got one: but these days *I* do what *he* tells *me*.

Will I have yet another last hunting season, what'll I ride... will Dandy be up to it, will *Horse & Hound* continue to employ me? I just don't know: those sorts of questions usually seem to answer themselves, I don't tend to push at them: we'll see. Have I become a fatalist?

THE barn dance wasn't a harvest home of course, it was a seventieth birthday party, but it was held in a magnificent old barn, which must have seen many harvest homes in the past. I went dreading it, determined not to dance, but in the event adored the evening and danced like a dervish. Virginia Reels, Stripping the Willow, you name it, we did it. When, exhausted, I decided to be a wallflower, it was such a joy just to watch: it is a rare pleasure to see dancers abandon themselves, just as it is to hear a good voice surrender to lyrical song. I didn't really want to go home, but, when we got there, other sounds of wild revelry came up to us across the vale.

"That's the wedding party", Diana said. Sure enough, next morning I could see the marquee, more than a mile away, on Boys Hill, where the old droveway runs. I could also, then, hear the sound of clapping and cheering from the direction of the village: a reminder that it was Iron Man day.

Iron Man (surely it ought to be 'Iron Person', somebody at County Hall must have slipped up?) is a triathlon in which those mad enough to take part have to swim three miles or so in Sherborne Castle's lake, bicycle goodness knows how many miles, Yeovil-Dorchester-Sherborne three times round, and run a full marathon. You have to admire them, but it didn't look much fun when Charlie carrying Stephie, and I walked down the drive to see them peddle furiously by.

The local roads were all closed, the village cut off from the outside world for half the day as if we had the plague: there was no possibility of holding a church service. To get away for our christening party we had to escape in the car over the fields, and hope to be able to talk our way across the cyclists' route at the far end of our journey, outside Dorchester.

In fact the event was admirably organised, but I reserve final judgement until I see whether or not the stewards have picked up the blizzard of yellow plastic water bottles that were still littering the Old Sherborne Road, the 'Top Road' as we call it, when we followed the by then empty cyclists' route home. (They did).

Another legacy of Iron Man was giant graffiti on the road leading out of the village, unintelligible coded messages of love and encouragement for the cyclists. Dandy took great exception to them when we rode by a couple of days later, inspecting them closely with lowered head, as though reading them, shying this way and that in his determination not to tread on them.

The lettering will wash off with rain I am told, and I believe it. Generally speaking Iron Man was rather a successful exercise in town-visits-country: I've changed from resenting it as an intrusion, to thinking it rather a good thing.

⤎⧳⤏

"IS SHE a chestnut mare, have I got that right?" Anna, who, like Charlie, is not horsy, asked me when I bought Bella into the kitchen yard one morning to show her to my baby granddaughter. I gave Anna the old line about what chestnut mares are said to have in common with red-headed women – my daughter-in-law is a brunette – she laughed, and asked me if Bella was expensive as well as thin-skinned and tricky.

Diana, who had rushed out of the kitchen to wrench from her jaws the plants that Bella was browsing, "They might be poisonous!", said that I had done well to persuade her through the wicket and into the narrow confines of the yard. I replied that Bella would follow me anywhere, which is no more than the truth: if she would only **take** me anywhere, had the nerve to match her ability, she'd be the horse of a lifetime, and any doubts about the coming hunting season would be taken care of.

August 25th.

"The hut stood on little wheels, which raised its floor about
a foot from the ground. Such shepherds' huts are dragged
into the fields when the lambing season comes on, to
shelter the shepherd in his enforced nightly attendance."

AS Dandy and I left the village an open gate beguiled me. I just could not pass it, nipped quickly out-of-sight round the corner of a wood, letting Dandy stretch his legs across newly mown grass. We had no business being there, but what harm, who would know? A tussle in an overgrown gateway, with the brambles I was cutting pulling one way and Dandy at the length of his reins pulling the other, left me with fingers like Jeremy Fisher's after his misadventure with the pike. But we made it through, off Tom Tiddler's ground, back to respectability, and went, with permission, to view my neighbour's new acquisition, his shepherd's hut.

It stood in a glade, deep in his wood, spot-lit by the sun, surrounded by Rosebay Willowherb; a lovely sight, and a lovely thing to own; a rustic version of a London cabbie's shelter; a bit of history.

Next stop, after another illicit seasonal stubble gallop was to check on a calf I had seen, newly born and looking sickly, the day before. Neither it nor its mama was with the other pregnant Jerseys. It had died I later learnt, and the mother, poor thing, was back in the dairy herd.

En route we had put up a flock of Canada geese feeding in the stubble – surely the word 'gaggle' doesn't do for eighty or more birds? They took off with much disgruntled honking in three great straggling skeins. Dandy didn't so much as falter in his stride at this, to me, quite unprecedented sight.

Nor did he turn a hair when, a few minutes later, we found ourselves suddenly surrounded by a pack of miscellaneous dogs, in full cry round his heels, yelping in his face, some even ducking underneath his belly. He's such a dear, so gentle, so stolid when he chooses, if only he could be relied upon to jump.

You must be wondering about the dogs, so indeed was I. It was by a stream we met them, and just for a moment, until I focussed on their complete jumble of breeds and sizes, I thought that it was a pack of mink hounds; that we had stumbled on a hunt.

No such thing. It was a lady called Jan whom I occasionally encounter walking her dog there, but who now, she told me, "Has dogs to stay". When I asked her how many were in her pack, she said, looking quickly round them, "I've only got ten here, there are more at home".

Despite their harmlessly mobbing Dandy, without any lead or whistle, she had remarkable control of them. Her cool and her command impressed me, but I couldn't help wondering what she did about the deer, the place is alive with them.

August 30th – September 12th.

AFTER a few happy days in Santa Marguerita Ligure, high up in the groin of Italy, and a night in Milan, we made a bandolier rail trip south across the peninsular, coast to coast, to Ancona, to catch the boat for Split. I don't recommend that ferry, unless you don't object to being cheated: I got the strong impression that it was run by a consortium of Italian Mafia and Croatian banditti. We'll fly next time.

Neighbour Robert was waiting for us on the jetty when a second, much shorter, much pleasanter, ferry trip delivered us to the island of Vis. Soon we were installed in our old quarters in his yacht Quicksilver, the boat we unforgettably helped him collect from her builders on Lake Erie, and which I so nearly put on the rocks in the River Hudson.

Vis is just full of beauty, history and interest. From earliest times, everybody has seemed to want to possess it, Greeks, Romans, Venetians, Turks, Austrians, Napoleon and Mussolini all had a go. For five years, 1810 to 1815, we were there. According to the guidebook, a proud read, *"The British Years* were the best and most prosperous in the island's history".

On one side or the anchorage an old ruined fort has George III's cipher on the keystone over its entrance. On the other is a walled cemetery in which I read the following inscription, left by a Brigadier Tom Churchill in 1944…

> "After more than one hundred years
> British Soldiers and Sailors
> who fought and died for their country's honour
> on the seas and islands of Dalmatia
> have again been laid to rest
> in this island cemetery."

> *"Here dead we lie because we did not choose*
> *to live and shame the land from which we sprung.*
> *Life to be sure is nothing much to lose*
> *But young men think it is, and we were young".*

You can perhaps imagine my feeling on stumbling on this, when exploring, quite unprepared. Somewhere else, I can't remember where, I read some lines written by one of our Commandos after surviving a particularly bloody engagement in the Adriatic, an attack on the neighbouring island of Brac, in World War II…

> "Death passed me by, but I caught his swift glance and knew,
> That he had seen me too."

I only wish that I could honour the writer by telling you who he was.

VIS was devastated by phylloxera in 1910, lost all its vines, and most of its population. It now very much relies on expatriates for income, yachting folk and tourists. There is quite a large British colony; Glanvilles Wootton has a foothold there.

When Julia was showing us over a ruined house that they had bought, my inquiring hand found a pistol, quite small, designed I would think for a lady's handbag, resting in some sort of crevice in the masonry, and beside it a tiny pencil.

Robert took charge of the pistol, but I have the pencil, here, in front of me now. It is barely an inch long, machine-sharpened, although I broke the lead, it was gold in colour, but with a black head, un-chewed.

Things talk: leastways they talk to me, pose questions. "Who last used that evidently treasured pencil, to write what, and when? Why did he, or, I suspect from the size of the pistol, she, use it right down so short that you can barely hold it to write, as I have so often seen a squaddie smoke a precious fag down to last quarter-inch?"

I keep that pencil by me in my 'toy box' on the kitchen seat. Like my knapped flint, it is a talisman. It is also a reminder of Vis, its embattled history, its un-named soldier poet and its warriors' graves.

VI

November 13th.

"At the going down of the sun..."

IT WAS one of those blind corners in life that you sometimes stumble on, which somehow seem to have a special meaning, seem to stick in the mind. Coming downstairs on the morning after Remembrance Sunday the poppy in the lapel of my father's old hunting jacket hanging in the hall caught my eye. As I reached out to take it, to scrunch it in my hand on its way to the bin, for a moment my small world stood still.

The coat is a story in itself, and the poppy always means a lot, but that morning there was a cloud hanging over us. I was supposed to be hunting in the Quantocks, but Diana had been suddenly recalled to Pool hospital; there was some question arising from a previous visit. She had not shown much concern, said that the summons was just routine caution; but it had occurred to me, waking in the small hours of that Monday morning, that the medics seemed in a great hurry to see her again, having given us just three days' notice of her appointment.

Was I staring into the abyss that I dare not think of? Naturally, I kept the question to myself, but, for half a morning, until the cloud was happily lifted, each passing minute had a leaden, nightmare quality.

∽∾

THE story of my father's old coat is soon told. It was made for him by Bernard Weatherill when I was five years old: he was in his first practice, at South Petherton, in Somerset, having just qualified as a doctor. In those days smart London tailors used to send journeymen round the country out of season: my father was measured, and the coat given its various fittings, in front of his own drawing room fireplace, as my mother used to tell me whenever she saw me in it.

However, the date on the label being June 25th 1938, he barely had a chance to wear it before war broke out. Not waiting to be enlisted, spurning the exemption that, as a doctor, he might have claimed, he took himself off for a soldier. The coat did its duty in its turn when peace came, and in due course was passed on to me: my father never knew old age.

We mere hunt followers have not worn scarlet, or *pink* if you prefer it, since the hunting 'ban', it is thought to be unnecessarily provocative: but the coat was downstairs, looking all of its age, for a reason. Rather late on the evening before hounds were due to meet here, on Tuesday in poppy week, Rory, our young Huntsman and Master, had telephoned. "We want you to wear that old coat of your father's you told us about at the Hunt

– 53 –

Dinner", he said.

It was a nicely judged and thoughtful compliment, but had me scurrying round, that night and the following morning. I had meant just to ride up quietly onto the hill in my own time and see what hounds were doing, after entertaining the expected mass of followers at our meet. Dandy was unclipped, still out at grass, filthy, and also, as you have learnt, under a cloud. What was more, none of my kit was ready for the sort of critical inspection it gets on these occasions; and the port and glasses were still sitting at the wine-merchants in Sherborne waiting to be collected.

Suddenly, instead of steady ordered calm it was all rush, rush, rush. But we made it, thanks to neighbours rallying round, and Diana's good management, everyone, mounted or on foot was offered a glass and a sausage-roll, and Dandy appeared, his mane plaited, as tidy as an unclipped horse still in his winter woollies could reasonably be... although I tried to keep his plaits, my plaits, out of view of the Pony Club Commissioner.

Soon after moving off with his hounds Rory, jumping out of a deep place, carried away the top rail of a boundary fence between two different land-holdings. There was stock on both sides, and I promised the anxious Damage Steward that I would mend the fence within the hour. We climbed onto Dungeon Hill, Dandy and I, watched and listened as the hunt and its music disappeared into the Blackmore Vale, then turned rather mournfully for home, I undoing his plaits the while. I don't expect to wear that old coat of my father's again.

REMEMBRANCE Sunday had been rather special. Thanks to a generous neighbour our War Memorial, previously on a cramped blind-corner site, has recently been spaciously and much more safely laid out, with a small lawn, seat and garden. For the first time, certainly in my recollection, we started the service, and observed the two minutes' silence there, before all walking up our drive to the church.

I had already been booked to read the lesson in church. But, on the Saturday night (another of those surprise late telephone calls) one of our two priests asked me if I would also lay a wreath at the Memorial and say 'the sentence'. I agreed of course, as one must, but it worried me that the village was over-dosing on just one of its parishioners, and that there were others as well if not far better qualified than me to share the occasion's honours.

This was a thought reinforced as I walked down the drive, bowler-hatted, medals a-clink, when the first person I saw in the group waiting at the Memorial was a local farmer, an old and valued friend and hunting companion, who had been a wireless operator in Lancaster bombers in World War II. Then in church – it was a benefice service, seven parishes making up the large congregation – there was at least one young man, just out of the army, with more and harder-earned medals than my meagre row of two.

I had a word that evening with the Rector – we'll get it right next year.

DRIVING to Pool next day, trying to keep my mind in blinkers, I thought of the many days' hunting Diana and I had enjoyed in the country that we were driving through. Bypassing Tolpuddle on the new trunk road, the serpentine edge of Piddle Wood was on our right above us, and away off to the left a stretch of country that we have had such fun in, Roger's Hill, the line of the old Roman road, lost in the fields but there for those who know what to look for, and, in the distance, Bere Down with its striking group of Scots Pines standing just above the hunt kennels, Elderton Clump – perhaps an old Drovers' mark, who knows? An enormous rainbow stood arched over the whole lovely familiar scene on the way home, and my carefree heart was dancing.

ONE morning towards the end of that week, riding my precious bane Bella, I met the latest arrival in the village, walking his dog, in a gateway. Can you believe it, having been 'senior officer' hereabouts for as long as I can remember I am to be ousted by an admiral?!

I had explained the situation to him at an earlier meeting, how actual rank isn't everything, and that age, seniority and length of service must be allowed for, he seemed to understand – nice chap I thought, and he owns a lurcher, an adorable bitch called Zulu. I'm sure that we will all settle down happily together: perhaps when he comes to retire from the Navy I'll be ready to 'retire' too.

I was aiming to ride the 'egg run', not to collect eggs but to pick up the litter I had noticed when Diana and I had ridden by the chicken farm earlier in the week. Trying to do the same thing on Dandy on the previous day I had been turned back, for the first time in my life, by the floodwater in the bridleway ford. A monsoon had struck us through the night, our remote tributary of the Caundle Brook was like a full-grown river.

Dandy had stepped into it boldly enough, after stooping to take his usual few sips, but within half a stride the water was up to his belly. I realized that it would be over the saddle mid-stream, and for the first time took in that the current there had a dangerous, powerful, hungry look to it. He nearly foundered as we turned. We both had had a fright, and retraced our steps chastened, and I hope, at least on my part, a fraction wiser.

When Bella and I got to the ford a day later the water was still deep, but there was no threat in it. Such an odd mixture of harum-scarum and trusting steadiness, she waded through without hesitating. She would jump a mile if a gnat should clear its throat in the hedge, or an unexploded cock-pheasant suddenly go off in the verge as we pass by.

WE HAD already seen a pair of deer, dancing away to safety as deer do, such a matchless sight, but as we came dripping out of the ford two very large whitish birds got up mid-field ahead of us. There was a chorus of disapproval from assembled rooks in a nearby stand of trees as the unwel-come visitors flew out of view.

I supposed they must have just been seagulls, but... but... but? It really annoys me when I cannot recognize the jizz of a bird. I then thought that they could possibly have been herons, but two flaps of their great wings are usually as instantly recognizable as a couple of bars of Beethoven; and anyway I usually see herons singly, not in pairs.

Back on the road, and heading for home, I dismounted, unfastened the carrier bag I always keep tied to the saddle Ds, and started to pick up the leavings of the feckless. Kennels Lane is not my 'pitch', but it had come to look a bit neglected, and who knows what casualty had prevented its regular, and usually very faithful, picker-upper from attending to it?

After a few paces I met Teresa from the egg farm walking her two spaniels. She told me something that made me very sad and reflective, and prepared me for the notice with a big red arrow by it that I read when I got to the egg farm gate. It said....

"To all our customers – it is with great regret that we shall cease to sell eggs from the end of November. This is due to a high number of thefts over the last six months, unreasonable expectations from the taxman, and health issues (Teresa had told me that Steve was getting gyp from his hips). *One thing at a time we can cope with, but not all three. Many thanks to all our customers who have stayed with us over the years, we shall miss our chats over the gate. We now hope to wind down towards retirement. Have a good Christmas, God Bless. Steve and Teresa."*

So thieves, chief amongst whom I count the Inland Revenue, have helped to drive this absolutely admirable small, hard-working enterprise out of business, and deprive the neighbourhood of a valued source of free-range eggs, laid by happy chickens. *Eheu!*

"Behold, I tell you a mystery...."

KENNELS Lane was in fact clearer of rubbish than I had feared to find it, but there was one new mystery, a badger skin lying squashed by the verge

– just the pelt, no bones or carcass, work that out! I made a mental note to go back with a dung-fork and heave it over the hedge where it could rot down out-of-sight, inoffensively, and Nature could do her work without the help of passing cars. I can't bear to see the once beautiful bodies of wild animals obscenely desecrated and spread about the road.

The final piece of litter to go into my bag was the poppy that still somehow had survived, pinned to my riding-jacket. "That's the last of them for another year" I thought..... until I went to lock up the church that evening. I had the forgotten my father's memorial.

Having lived through two wars, and having served in one, my father cared a great deal about the British Legion and Remembrance Day. So, greatly daring, a few years back, I had hammered a small wire staple into the mortar below his wall tablet, so that he might, as it were, continue to sport a poppy every year, hoping that, as I held the guilty hammer in my hand, I didn't need to apply to the Diocese in Salisbury for a 'faculty'.

When, just out of the Army, as Church Warden, I had been so wicked as to modernize the antique and useless heating system in our church, somehow, I forget how, raising the necessary large sum of money, I was punished by being hauled in front of the Chancellor of the Diocese in a Consistory Court, for not getting the proper paper permission, the so-called faculty.... such nonsense!

We won our case in court, but it meant that our new heating system cost a few hundred pounds more than it need have done, in legal fees. It's un-Christian I know, but I never can nor ever will forgive the hierarchy for that piece of blinkered bureaucratic foolishness; that, and for undervaluing our precious old liturgy and the King James Bible. I think of them as a bunch of well-meaning nitwits, who...

> *"Like the base Indian, threw a pearl away*
> *Richer than all his tribe..."*

I SOLVED the mystery of the badger skin, at least to my own satisfaction, by ringing my old friend our late Rector, now retired down Exmoor way. "Oh, I've often eaten badger" he said, "hot and cold. The Seavington Hunt used to hold regular Badger Suppers when I was a boy".

It's not that long since I found the four lower legs of an ox dumped in a sack in the bed of the stream that runs by Kennels Lane, then, later, the heads and feet of two roe deer similarly discarded. It is evidently on the rat-run of some low-life amateur butcher, as well as of egg-thieves.

> *"Age shall not weary them..."*

TIME and again these days we are reminded by the broadsheet obituary pages of those who saw service in World War II but were left to grow old amongst us... for whom they did so much. As another Remembrance

Sunday faded into memory, and the poppy wreath that I had laid on our memorial headed for the bin, it seems a good moment to salute the parting figures of my parents' generation, and to take stock of the legacy they left behind.

How often in recent years has one not read, with widening eyes, of the unbelievable courage and uncomplaining hardihood of yet another of that breed? It might perhaps be someone who has lived quietly amongst us, his or her heroism forgotten before its final brief comet blaze across a newspaper page brings us up short with a mixture of pride, regret... and shame. Shame that we had not made more of them, and, looking around us, shame that perhaps we have not made the best use of the freedom they so tenaciously and selflessly defended.

One such saw out his retirement, with his wife, a one-time WRNS officer, running our saddler's shop in Sherborne, where, if needs be, he never minded himself turning his hand to cutting and stitching leather. Born in 1921, he entered Dartmouth in the year the war started and volunteered for submarine service. He had already earned a DSC and Polish Cross of Valour when, aged 22, in September 1943, he took his midget submarine X7 with its two tons of explosive into a Norwegian fiord.

Overcoming incredible underwater hazards and misadventures, he and his crew of three, managed so to cripple the German battleship *Tirpitz* that she never took to sea again. X7 and two of her crew were lost, but he and one crewman saw out the war in captivity. After that war, before retiring, he flew Sea Furies off the aircraft carrier *Glory* in the Korean War.

Rear-Admiral Godfrey Place VC died in 1994, and that was when, God rest his warrior soul, most of us, his Dorset neighbours, who had so often passed the time of day with him in his Cheap Street shop, perhaps delivering some disreputable piece of tack for repair "as soon as possible please", first learned the full details of his war record.

Though the numbers falter and thin out, there is no end, still, to that parade of World War II heroes, those men and women who troop through the obituary pages, and have been duly *'honoured in their generations, and were the glory of their times'*. But what of those many thousands who did their humble bit but have no such memorial? May I be allowed to tell the story that I know best, that of my own parents and a favourite uncle?

AS I have already mentioned – please forgive my boasting of it – as soon as war broke out my father volunteered, joined the RAMC, serving out the greater part of his war at sea on troop ships. Remember the U boats? He never spoke to me of them: to my shame I never asked. He had to abandon ship once only, and it is a question whether or not my mother had a harder war. With three small children – house, servants, all accustomed comforts suddenly gone – it was truly a case of *'Goodbye to All That'*.

She had to lead a gypsy life, moving from rooms, to lodgings, to various rented temporary homes, teaching herself housework and cooking, and making shift as best she could. One such temporary home, a mill house in Essex, was demolished by a stray bomb whilst she slept. She, my sister and my grandmother, were fortunate to escape alive; my brother and I were at boarding school by then. But we were a lucky family; both of my parents survived the war to pick up the threads of peacetime life again.

⤜✿⤛

IN THE final week of May 1940 word went round the City, where my uncle worked, that everything that could float was needed off the beaches of Dunkirk. He had seen service in the trenches in World War I. I have a picture of him, seated cross-legged like a schoolboy at the feet of his CO, Winston Churchill, then out of office and briefly commanding the 6th Royal Scots Fusiliers.

In 1940 Mathew Hackforth-Jones was too old for active service, but not for sailing. I don't know how many cross-channel trips he made in those hectic dangerous days, but the picture of that brave flotilla of small boats with its superannuated crews leaving the home shore to help rescue their country's beleaguered army is a telling one.

Almost every day now, as we may read in the obituary columns, without noise, self-advertisement, celebrity or fuss, as ever was their way, the last remnants of another great armada for the last time, one by one, cast off, quit the home shore and sail away.

"... and in the morning, we will remember them".

BY THE way, in case you didn't twig that I was joking, about our new neighbour the admiral, here's what I said on the subject of being by mistake taken seriously, when I had to address the Surtees Society after their annual dinner, on the subject of 'Sporting Journalism Then and Now'...

"It is my view that, along with many of those who have the misfortune to be born fiddle-faced, not much given to geniality or small talk, Surtees often had his irony taken at face value. This is a Pooh trap, for ever at the feet of those not born affable. I should know: I recently wrote an article on treacle-mining, and had it taken seriously in some quarters.... It was for an April issue."

.... Being unintentionally taken seriously is the only characteristic that I claim to have in common with that great man Robert Smith Surtees (1806-1864), creator of Jorrocks, the hunting grocer – his dates are generally given wrongly in reference books, so don't rush to correct me.

I was addressing his worshipers in his 200th anniversary year, and a great and terrifying honour it was, standing in front of a full-length portrait of Winston Churchill, after a miserably uncomfortable and seemingly endless dinner, in the Carlton Club, in St James's Street. As I have said often before, I'm never going to agree to give an after-dinner speech ever again.

More on the serious subject of treacle-mining, another day.

"… and immediately there fell from his eyes as it had been scales".

ALL OF us must surely know the feeling of having a sudden 'moment of truth', but how often does it happen twice in a single day? Dandy had got a bit above himself, had been giving Diana, for whom he is quite unsuited, but whom I dare not risk on tricky Bella's back, a hard time. So, one December morning, I set out to get to the bottom of him, give him some really hard work that would sober him up, at least for a few days: he is such a bovver boy.

This meant riding up to the ridge-way, and we set off, with permission, through Robert's Wood, jumping a fairly respectable fallen tree trunk on our way. He took it beautifully, quite in his old style, which was rather sad in the light of what was to follow.

Coming down off the ridge above Buckland Newton, well on our way home, he tried to get away from me at the gallop. That was nothing new. But then, when I had him steadily cantering, in hand, on smooth pasture, he stumbled heavily, grossly – it was sheer clumsiness, there was no excuse for it. Typically of an Irish horse, he found his 'fifth' leg, where another horse might have fallen, but the jar caught me painfully in the back, where I crushed a couple of vertebrae thirty years ago when another cloth-footed horse did its best to kill me.

In that moment it came to me, with undeniable force, that I didn't want to hunt Dandy any more, that he was too headstrong and clumsy, that I was finished with him. It was rather a sad ride home. Diana didn't actually say "I told you so!", but the truth is that she had been telling me just that for months, that it was long since time I got myself a more suitable horse.

～∞～

THE second blinding flash of the obvious came when I was reading the newspaper in the kitchen at lunchtime. There was a long, and very moving account of how the parents of one of the casualties in Iraq, the hundredth of our soldiers killed in that doubtful theatre, were bravely battling with their grief, coping with what Thomas Hardy called, *'the inevitable movement onward'* that must, if we are to survive, follow even the worst tragedy.

I read "When Tony Blair visited the troops in Basra before Christmas last year (2005), Gordon amused his parents by recounting how the PM repeated his descent from the boat *seven* times to perfect the photograph". I for a moment imagined myself, again, visiting troops in an operational situation – I have done it, often enough, but never in a true war zone, never in anything like the conditions our troops face in Iraq – and thought, how could it be possible for a man to sink so low as to pose for the cameras, repeatedly, Narcissus-like, when his business was visiting soldiers in the field, and the only thought in his mind should have been for *their* concerns, *their* situation and *their* welfare; what on earth did he think *they* were thinking, or did he just not care?

Truly, the man, and anyone like him in his trade if he was merely doing what they all do, has neither pride nor shame: indeed it is as good an example as I have come across yet of what I call, and mourn, 'the death of shame'. I had never quite thought of our Prime Minister, or politicians generally, in that light before.   Compassion battles with contempt: how could a man who should be great, be made by the conditions of his work and the exigencies of modern public life so utterly despicable and small?

"It's Tommy this, an' Tommy that...
...we serve no red-coats here".

CHARLES Moore, a favourite columnist wrote, on the day following, in support of the *Daily Telegraph's* Christmas charity SSAFA (bless them), of how the armed services were undervalued by a society that now hardly knows anything about them. He told of how two Royal Marines, attending a funeral of one of their colleagues in Liverpool, were refused admission to a bar because they were in uniform.

"Soldiers, sailors and airmen do the most astonishing things on our behalf" he wrote, "and we neither know or care very much... there are fewer than a quarter of a million people in the Services, so the majority of civilians do not know any servicemen personally".

Exactly! I can't fault that sentiment, except perhaps, having a niece not long back from serving in Iraq, I wish that he had somehow mentioned servicewomen. "Because the 20th century was one of total war" he wrote, "everyone knew something of what it is to be in the Services... (now there is a)…. sense of separation"… between society and the Armed Services".

I had recently had a stark if comic reminder of that separation, and the ignorance, perhaps it would be kinder to say the innocence, which stems from it.

Startling symptoms in an eye had sent me on a rare visit to the doctor, who sent me on post-haste to hospital. It wasn't a detached retina, it was something quite harmless, but which shares its symptoms, called a Weiss Ring – say that aloud to yourself and you will smile – something floating around inside the eye that would eventually of its own accord go away.

The point of my story is that the absolutely charming nurse who tested my eyesight before the consultant saw me, said hesitatingly, and with the sweetest possible smile and blushes. "I hope you don't mind my asking... but we have been wondering in the office... what does this word 'brigadier' mean, we've never come across it before?".

"It's an army rank, like lance-corporal" I replied, whilst struggling not to look down into the vertiginous, totally unsuspected chasm that had suddenly opened at our feet between her world, her generation, and my own. Has 'common knowledge' really shrunk to the compass of a pinhead? How right Charles Moore was in his article: this was, by the way, for me, yet another 'moment of truth'.

(It came to me some weeks later when I was digging the vegetable garden, the way inconsequential thoughts will arrive unbidden at odd moments, that it might come in quite useful one day, this ignorance of Army ranks. I know what I shall say when I next land up in hospital in answer to the question "What's your first name then duckie?".)

A word about SSAFA (the Soldiers, Sailors, Airmen and Families Association), and why I bless both them, and the *Daily Telegraph* for supporting them. If you have ever been responsible for the welfare of troops far away from their roots, have tried, albeit as an almost beardless young man, to be some sort of father to them, wrestled daily with their worries about troubles at home, the latest 'Dear John' letter from a girl-friend etc, you will no doubt have blessed SSAFA too. Recalling my time as a troop and squadron leader in far off places I just cannot thank them enough.

VII

December 24th – 30th.

"Winter Holiday".

DO TODAY'S children read Arthur Ransome? It seems rather unlikely, but, if they do, they are surely stocking their memories for life with the doings and excitements of the Blackett and Walker children, the 'Swallows and Amazons'. The title of the book in which John, Titty and Co build an ice-yacht came back to me strongly as we waited anxiously to get away for a week's skiing over Christmas 2006.

For some reason, I had never looked forward to a holiday as intensely as I did that winter, or, so it seemed, never counted on the break as much. Yet the country was under fog for a week, Heathrow was in chaos, and there was said to be no snow in the Alps. Would we get away, would we be able to get on our skis if we did?

We were due to fly out with Melanie, and my eight-year-old playmate, Jasper, joining Louise and her family, and base ourselves on the apartment that she and her Italian husband Massimo had recently bought in Verbier.

∽∾∾

WE HAD a rather unusual engagement on the night before leaving, it was Duffy Fox our farrier's sixtieth birthday party. His wife had rung me in great secrecy some weeks earlier; there was much covert e-mail traffic too with Duffy's daughter. It was to be a surprise party.

Knowing how impossible it is to keep a secret in a family, it was small surprise to me when, one day whilst he was shoeing Dandy, the birthday boy told me himself, with many a sly smile, and in some detail, what was planned. He hadn't let-on that he knew all about the 'surprise' of course: for my part, I also feigned ignorance. With all the bluff and double-bluff we seemed to be taking a journey into Le Carré country.

Duffy originally enlisted in the Army as a drummer-boy. Some time ago he started a folk song-and-dance group called Stampede, it has been a great success, raises money for charity (£1000 in the previous year), is much in demand. His wife Merrill, who has with a little help taught herself to play the fiddle, got up the Appalachian dance group. The cover-plan for the surprise birthday party was that it was just another of Stampede's gigs, the date a pure coincidence – I don't think somehow that Merrill would have got very far in the Secret Service.

If I say that Diana and I were slightly doubtful as we made the long car journey south that evening, through the remnants of the fog, to beyond Weymouth, it was nothing to do with the occasion. It was because our minds were on our packing, on an early start next day, and the questions hanging over our precious, longed for but threatened, brief skiing holiday – although the fog did at last seem to be lifting.

Strange, isn't it, how the best parties catch you by surprise – and the ones most eagerly anticipated so often disappoint? How can I convey to you what fun the dancing and the music were? It was a bit like square-dancing, but without a caller, and with a lot of noisy shoe-work. Appalachian dancers, dressed as farm girls, so obviously enjoy it all, it's so smiley, innocent, and catchy, it knocks spots off 'me-me' moaning pop, it's so happy.

There were strong echoes also, of another world, courageous settlers getting together for a hoedown to enjoy themselves, making the best of a hard life long ago and far away. Reminders of Leatherstocking country, *The Last of the Mohicans* and all that, up-state New York, where Diana and I once unforgettably helped crew *Quicksilver* from her builders on Lake Eerie, through the Appalachians via the Clinton Canal with its famous lock-system to the Hudson, where I did my incompetent best to wreck her.

The venue for the party was a converted barn, part of a farm on Chesil shore at East Fleet – remember *Moonfleet*, the classic smugglers tale? During a break in the music, one of the dancers came and knelt mysteriously by my chair. Would I sign a copy of my book? It was a Christmas present for the patron of the place, her father-in-law, who stood nearby superintending the buffet – hence the secrecy.

I've seldom enjoyed a party more: we could happily have stayed for hours.

∽∞∾

THE previous week had been torture – but then, the fog lifted, and, on the day we left, the *Daily Telegraph* carried a letter from someone in Verbier saying that it was all nonsense about the lack of snow. Over the letter was printed a picture of the slopes above Les Ruinettes: I actually felt a ridiculous tug of homesickness, a longing to be up there, a determination to be on that snow and on those familiar slopes at the very earliest moment possible.

We flew out on Christmas Eve. By 11am next day, having hired skis and bought a five-day pass, I was looking down guiltily on Verbier's church tower from Les Attelas (9,000 feet), with all the time in the world to ski down to the 'village' (it's a town really), for lunch, the grandchildren (step-grandchildren really), crackers, the Christmas tree, opening presents, and all that. I got onto my skis, and yes, in the long gap since Easter they hadn't forgotten what was expected of them, I could still 'ride a bicycle'. Down we went.

My skiing is much like my hunting. Being no great shakes as an athlete, I leave it to the skis. Sometimes they do foolish things, especially after lunch, but mostly they look after me in a sober, workmanlike if unadventurous fashion, get me down the mountain in one piece somehow. Skiing is a liberation, a joy, like sprouting wings, and is totally, utterly addictive. I had such a happy, selfish, naughty (not going to church), Christmas.

IF YOU are wondering about the horses, they were still unclipped, in their thick winter woollies, still living out. Our kind neighbour Sue was feeding them, checking the water-trough for ice, and generally mothering them. As has been the case for several years now, I had been uncertain whether or not I would hunt at the start of the new season, and, anyway, this time round, Dandy looked not to be up to it.

The matter was settled by *Horse & Hound* who asked me to 'do' this hunt, then that hunt, then another, and already, by Christmas, I had behind me three of the best rides I could have hoped for, on such different, characterful, competent horses, with already a couple of engagements stacked up for the New Year, with the promise of more to follow. Life seemed very good as I slid blithely down the mountain in my inexpert way, quite often wondering about Dandy and Bella who take up such a chunk of my normal everyday thoughts.

You don't see much wildlife on the mountain, although there is every sign of it in the spoor in the snow beneath you as you travel up the lifts. I saw a golden eagle, and a bunch of choughs, and that was about it. But human life, at its best and worst is all there – the helping hand when you fall, the idiot on the snowboard who knocks you over, hit and run.

It sticks in my mind that, on a rather steep bit above Les Ruinettes, where, for the first time, I heard the unwelcome rasp of bare ice under my skis, I passed a young woman looking miserable, nerve suddenly gone, paralysed by fear, too frightened to move or turn. Further down the slope I passed her boyfriend staring impatiently back, all too palpably, at that very moment, falling out of love with his Chelsea belle.

IS THIS a good moment I wonder to get something off my chest about nerve? I want to write something about it, but it's a tricky subject to embark on, for a man, especially for a soldier, who is supposed to be born brave. However I feel that I have something useful say about it – useful that is for people, boys particularly, who are afraid of being afraid, and, worst of all, afraid of showing fear. "Little boys can be such wimps" Diana had said, a day or so later, albeit with great kindness and understanding in her voice, when four-year-old Alexander failed to join his twin sister on the nursery slopes for a skiing lesson. In fact he's a little tough, not a wimp at all, and was skiing like a good 'un just a few days later.

But my very earliest memory is of, at exactly Alexander's age, being too frightened to jump off an orchard wall, being taunted mercilessly by my older brother for cowardice, crying out for help, being rescued and lifted down by Nanny. It would be ridiculous to say that it scarred me for life, but, as you can see, I have not forgotten it.

I was no good at games as a child, fell badly and hurt easily, had, still have, no natural sense of timing or balance, or spring in my stride, have never been able to throw a cricket ball, or run fast: I was what my fellow schoolboys unkindly but justly called 'a weed', the word 'wimp' hadn't been invented; even my sister was better than me at games, and got picked before me when teams were being made up.

A great part of the attraction of riding for me has been that horses lend you their athleticism, and their courage, just as skis lend you agility and speed. Learning the freedom that riding gives, was like coming suddenly on a hidden door. But, all through my boyhood I was haunted by the thought that I might not measure up, if the test should come. "Cowardy, cowardy custard, he won't jump off the wall!" my brother, now long dead, had sung. He was not consciously being unkind, was just being a boy.

Confidence came as I grew up, various challenges came my way, and I survived them. It is no small source of amusement to me that, now, in my seventies, people often call me 'brave' because, in my work as a hunting correspondent, I have to ride all sorts of strange horses. I don't find that that requires courage at all, I love horses, and they seem to quite like me. I'm not frightened so cannot deserve to be called brave, it is pure pleasure, the horses that I am given to ride being so capable and sympathetic.

But I always have been, and still am, aware of my nerves when I ride, especially riding at speed, and across country: it is part of the pleasure, overcoming one's natural fear. I think what I am trying to say to nervous 'weedy' boys, such as I was, is "Have patience, we are not all born with the taste or skill for the Cresta run, or to win the Victoria Cross. Trust yourself, test yourself, *take* courage: the manliness that you need to get through life will surely come".

THERE had been a crescent moon high in the sky, lying almost on its back, like a puppy asking to have its tummy tickled, during the long coach journey round Lake Geneva, from that city's airport to Verbier, when we arrived on Christmas Eve. On the last day of our holiday the moon was half-full, and tipping forward, as if tipsy, on tiptoes, looking naughtily down a corsage. It was there, above the jagged skyline, as I took almost the first lift up the mountain, determined to get every minute's skiing daylight gave.

There was just one set of tracks on the freshly smoothed piste when I reached it, and I had the whole of a vast expanse of pristine snow virtually to myself, the sun still off-stage behind a frieze of peaks, promising an early entry from the wings had yet to find the valley bottom. The snow under my skis was crisp, but both holding and giving – perfect snow in fact.

I sang, as I often do when I am at home, riding out of earshot, this time, to suit the occasion, such snatches as I could remember of the Prize Song from Wagner's *Die Meistersinger.* To my mind one of the greatest tunes in all opera, it begins *"Morgenlicht leuchtend..."* – morning is dawning – and ends, hauntingly, when properly sung *"...in Paradies".* I was conscious that I was living a moment that I would not soon, if ever, forget, and being reminded again of why I leave just a little bit of my Dorset heart behind me every time I quit the Alps.

THE mad Englishman abroad, I had been up too sharp for the convenience of the hotel staff at breakfast, and I was much too early to get more than a surly welcome at the cabin at the bottom of that opening run when I demanded my first *chocolat chaud* of the day. They were all busy shouting at each other, as chefs will, and making a fiendish din with outsize mixing machines: it's just as well not to see too much of what goes on backstage in such places, I marked it down mentally as a spot at which not to break for lunch that day.

Diana, who, taking time off from being an unselfish granny, had joined me for half the morning, said as we parted, "Don't do anything silly, we don't want you breaking your leg on the last day!". Over a solitary lunch I had a bit of a battle with my conscience as to whether or not what I had privately planned for the afternoon was 'silly'. I aimed to venture higher, out of the area of my ski-pass, towards Mont Fort.

The queue in the self-service restaurant back at Les Attelas was moving so slowly, and the chance to get to windward of the mercenary Swiss so very rare, that when, finding myself for some time stationary in front of the *vin chaud* urn, on the sly I emptied and refilled my glass a couple of times, or so. This seemed to have got to my skis, which were quite out of sorts, inept, a bit chicken even, when I resumed them. "Mont Fort? Definitely no!" I said to myself, as we fudged yet another turn, descending on suddenly difficult snow, the same that had seemed so friendly in the morning.

But, as you have probably already guessed, by the time we reached the decisive fork my skis and I felt more ourselves. We switched our down-hill course into the adjoining valley, and headed guiltily for the forbidden lift.

IF THEY are mercenary, grittily determined that you shall leave the mountains with an empty wallet, the French-speaking Swiss are generous with their charm. It is Gallic charm, sadly so rare in much of France today, and it is charm happily allied to Teutonic competence. Truly you have the best of two worlds when you ski above the Rhône in the Four Valleys.

It was therefore no surprise to me when the young lady in the kiosk at the Mont Fort funicular laughed prettily when, removing my woolly hat to show the colour of my hair, I said "As you can see, I am very old, how much supplement must I pay for one ascent?" "Non, non Monsieur, vous êtes trés jeune, huit francs   ...'ow-evair, you must go immédiatment, it ees ze last leeft". £4 didn't seem too much to pay for being wafted up another thousand feet. The sun was indeed at tip-toes on its diving board, I hastened on.

There weren't many of us to clatter and shuffle in our heavy boots out of that last lift at the Col de Gentianes, and, such as there were flicked off down the mountainside with disconcerting speed. I could for once have done with company.

It was in fact, apart from the snow coverage being patchy, an easy run, the route well marked, a long, long snake, a road I guess in summer, with the occasional option of quitting the track to descend direct from one of its loops to another. Here and there, where the snow was worn on the track's sharp corners, some sort of straw had been helpfully put down: I had never skied on straw before, it took skis well.

There was also a litter of loose rock and stones to be avoided. Just occasionally, if you were careless where you went, searching for a view of Mont Blanc perhaps, or checking how close the sun was to its high horizon, a bare patch of earth or stone would grab the skis from behind, arresting their smooth progress – the sensation is like treading on the wrong pedal in an automatic car, you are thrown forward, suddenly, jarringly, your wandering mind called immediately to order.

It was a long run. Like the first run of the morning, it seemed stolen in its improbable, precious and unforgettable beauty, in its stillness and so privileged, if slightly scary solitude. At the bottom of that same high valley where my day had started, I quit. Sadly, slightly guiltily as when one leaves hounds when they are running, I took the lift up, out of the valley, and over and all the way down to Verbier, knowing that I had had the best of a memorable, exhausting day, that it would indeed be 'silly' not to stop.

There were still upright black ants descending Ruinettes, nothing looks quite so like an ant as the distant figure of a skier, but the sun was a burnished penny, already halfway into its moneybox. It was fully time for home.

DURING the lead-up to our Christmas break I had been busy working on an article for the April issue of *The Field* on 'swimming squirrels', a sequel to the piece that had come out in the previous April on 'Treacle Mining', and which had caused quite a stir. I had had no idea when I originally suggested the first piece to the Editor, after stumbling on a 'treacle well' on a chance visit to Burton Bradstock, that it would lead me the dance it did.

He replied to my e-mail "Ah, the treacle mining.... I think that it all started with an old friend of my family's... who... was squire of Dunchideock and mined treacle there as far back as I can remember.... Let's pursue the idea, though I think your friend's recent discovery of a treacle well in Dorset will have to take a back seat to the older deposits in Devon! Let's talk more".

"Small world!" I thought "I'd never heard of treacle mining before, yet he seems to know all about it". I suppose that I should have read more than I did into his exclamation mark, but the scientific rational for treacle deposits, and all the stuff on the internet, being quite convincing: from that moment, for a week or so, I wasn't entirely sure who was kidding whom. It seemed that I had entered a shadow world full of distorting mirrors. I didn't even know for sure if my Editor was being serious.

I got my feet eventually onto firm ground by going back to Burton Bradstock, asking the Rector, who was becoming quite a friend, to take me down his tunnel to his treacle well, and putting a straight question to him. He turned to me, saying nothing but with a beatific smile that told me all that I required to know. From that moment the article was plain sailing and great fun to write. Where I found gaps in the 'evidence' I just used my imagination, made it up, as one must occasionally now-a-days as a Hunting Correspondent.

If, as you read the piece, you find yourself at all lost, wondering what is fact and what is fiction, as I was when I first entered on the subject, I invite you to take a close look at the *names* cited, say them over to yourself, study them, starting perhaps with Dr Unkard.

"Play it absolutely straight" the Editor had ordered, but I thought it only kind to leave my trusting readers a trail of gentle clues to the fact that, from start to finish, I had my fingers firmly crossed behind my back. Here's what I wrote...

"IT WAS when I found myself in the village of Burton Bradstock, in the far west of Dorset, one day late last summer that I first began to think of treacle mining, and treacle wells, as anything more than a typically extravagant piece of Lewis Carroll fantasy. You probably remember that a treacle well featured in the Dormouse's rather inconclusive story at the

Mad Hatter's tea-party in *Alice in Wonderland* – three sisters, Elsie, Lacie and Tillie, lived at the bottom of one.

What you perhaps don't know - as I didn't until recently - unless you happen to live in that part of the world, is that Lewis Carroll was writing about a real treacle well, which was, and still is, in the churchyard of St Margaret's, in Binsey, Oxfordshire, no distance from Christ Church College where Lewis Carroll was a mathematics don.

What you certainly won't know, unless you take *The Pharmaceutical Journal*, and have studied the issue of March 12th last year, is that 'the medicinal balm known as theriaca… in Middle English tryacle or treacle… was recommended by the Royal College of Physicians… when in 1665 the Great Plague ravaged London. Apparently Binsey is still ranked among the country's treacle wells, and it is claimed that children are encouraged to draw therapeutic treacle from its depths by means of a jar attached to a string'.

Treacle mines exist, I learn from the same source, in thirteen different counties across England – Cumbria, Devon, Essex, Gloucestershire, Hampshire, Kent , Lancashire, Leicestershire, Norfolk, Surrey, Sussex and Wiltshire: there are no fewer than nineteen treacle mines or wells in Oxfordshire alone.

The geological origin of naturally occurring treacle, similar to that of coal, is beds rich in the fossil remains of primitive forms of sugar cane trapped deep underground in rock formations, millions of years ago: the ubiquitous weed Mare's Tail is the nearest equivalent in the present day English flora. History does not record when miners first chanced on it: certainly the Romans mined treacle in this country, and valued it enormously: probably its extraction goes back to well before that, into Bronze-age if not Neolithic times.

Burton Bradstock owes its treacle deposits to the geological formations on which the village stands. Just outside Bridport, at the start of the long sweep of Chesil Beech, it is in the heart of what one writer has called "the id of Dorset's psyche" – that most magic and varied of litoral tracts, the Jurassic Coast, stretching from Lulworth to Lyme, from Purbeck to Golden Cap.

When I visited, Burton had just had its annual Church Fête. The village's recently rediscovered treacle well was the prize exhibit. Enormous queues had formed to inspect the site, and to carry away small jars of its honeyed exudate: the Fête enjoyed a record attendance.

The well, I learnt, had been re-discovered in a quite unique feature of the Rector's garden. One of his predecessors, in Victorian times one supposes, had been so offended by the sight of his maidservants tripping to and from the earth closet at the bottom of the rectory garden that he had a tunnel constructed, the full length of the lawn, so that their visits might indeed be privy."

"DUNCHIDEOCK'S famous treacle mine, or I should say mines – there are two of them – have of course a much longer history than has the recently discovered well at Burton Bradstock. The latter, though under-ground, and reached via a tunnel, is merely a well, that is to say the treacle is recovered by being scraped off the walls of the well chamber. At Dunchideok, slag, which must be processed, is excavated by the miners: it is a much larger scale operation.

One of the first things I was shown on arrival was a sample of this 'cake' as it is called. It is a black substance, sponge-like in appearance, but crumbly to the touch, and with an aroma that took one straight back to the nursery, memories of toasting forks, and that slightly disturbing image on the Golden Syrup tin of a lion, dead or asleep, under a cloud of bees. 'Out of the strong came forth sweetness' the legend read, but Nanny couldn't exactly explain why.

Dunchideock, mining apart, is otherwise a farming parish, a few miles west of Exeter, concealed, as so many Devon villages blissfully are, amongst small, steep hills, and approached via thread-needle lanes. The mine I was to visit was beneath the principal house in the place, where I was hospitably welcomed, and where the Clerk to the Mines told me something of the mine's history.

It has been worked, I learned, since medieval times, and prospered until the imposition of a punitive tax in 1781. Since then modern methods of synthesizing treacle have driven out older skills, and inferior, cheaper maple syrup has stolen the market. I was reminded of hearing a similar story in Manaus, in Amazonia, of how the rubber tree once promised unimaginable wealth to the forest dwellers of Brazil until we learnt how to cultivate rubber in Malaya.

Treacle is still extracted in this, the smaller of the two mines at Dunchideock, but for a very specialized, medical, market, and part time – the Clerk himself is a busy young farmer. "I just don't know where we would be without Dunchideock Treacle", Dr Unkard of Dart Pharmaceuticals told me, "it is the vital ingredient of all our standard sur-gical dressings, as well as of the humble corn-plaster".

Once underground, my first impression was of the cramped confines of the approach to the mine-face, and of the need to crouch low as I walked. Entering the mine I had the misfortune to strike my head, hard, against a dangling "Mind Your Head" sign: it was quite difficult, at first, to take in my surroundings for the stars.

However I was soon able to make out an impressive display of various ancient pieces of miners' equipment in the antechamber, and what, in my ignorance, I first took for wine-bins, since they looked exactly like the stone bins in my own cellar at home. They were in fact 'cooling racks' I was informed, and indeed they contained a complicated entanglement of metal shelving no doubt designed for that purpose.

I would have liked to have penetrated deeper into the mine, but my guide was understandably in a hurry to get back to his farm. There was however time for him to show me, and for me to touch, the dark, viscous walls of the furthest chamber that time allowed us to visit, and to sample the undeniable smell of the substance that has made Dunchideock so famous.

I was lucky enough however to find the other local mine open and working. In the fields over towards the neighbouring village of Doddiscombsleigh, totally concealed in a deep combe almost until you are on top of it, is an impressive complex, an altogether bigger operation, as the treacle-ore, or cake, is processed on site, for dispatch direct to inland and overseas markets.

The Mine Captain, Will Arthog – a name that betrays his Cornish origins, he moved to Devon on the closure of the last tin mine – after equipping me with a helmet, "Can't be too careful about Health and Safety these days", he confided with a wink, took me straight to the adit entrance. In no time we were more than a hundred paces into the hillside: "You're just in time", he told me, "they are going off shift this minute".

Sure enough, soon a gentle rumbling vibration came up the rails at our feet, and the ghostly near-white face of a pony hove into view. Meeting a horse underground was new experience. "We use the Dartmoor/Percheron cross" Arthog continued, "they live above ground of course, and this lead pony, Percival, will be out as usual with the Silverton Hunt with my daughter on board on Saturday".

We flattened ourselves against the, as I later discovered, rather sticky adit wall as Percival, leading a string of six, plodded past, each drawing a trolley heaped with the wholesome smelling cake. They were followed by a group of miners, among whom I fell in with Syd Ossage and Mike Ash, who told me that they had just completed six hours 'at the face'. "What was it like, mining treacle?" I asked – "Hard work" Syd replied, "but you get to like it, the cake, unlike some mineral ore, is pleasant stuff to handle". "You can overdose on the smell though" Mike added, "six hours of it is quite enough in twenty-four, and there's the wife and bairns at home to think of".

On regaining the surface I was shown round the refining shed where, making full use of the steep slope of the hillside, the ore is tipped direct into a hopper at the head of a massive cylindrical retort, from the base of which the refined product is eventually drawn, under clinical conditions, for sealing in small jars and wadkins. There is no waste-product I learnt, the slag, or 'slack' as it is called, is sold in all the local garden centres as mulch.

As we watched, we could actually hear Percival and his comrades tipping their loads into the hopper high above us, whilst, at the lower level, white-coated laboratory staff were busy, packaging and labelling the previous day's processed take. It was good to be able to see the whole process in a single comprehensive view.

"Viscosity used to be a major problem" one of my guides told me, "natural treacle has the highest surface tension of any substance known to man. What we call 'clean closure' in the decanting process was next to impossible, until the advent of modern laser technology. Working here, on the wadkin floor, used to be a very mucky job".

That Real Treacle, as it is known in the trade, has a wide and ready market is clear enough. Albert Ross, Marketing Manager of the Phine Phood deli and health-food chain, told me "It just flies off our shelves, it's a case of find it if you can". Why I wondered did supply limp along so lamely behind demand?

Vick Ermin, Senior Environmental Strategic Outreach Diversity Overview Co-ordinator at DEFRA, had the answer. "The Dunchideock treacle extraction facilities, like similar facilities all over the country, have to match out-take to resource availability, and to environmental factors. I must not anticipate the Minister's official announcement on TESAP, the Treacle Extraction Strategic Action Plan, due to be rolled out shortly, but treacle has to take its due place in the scheme of things. We cannot allow treacle extraction to prejudice the prime purpose of this area, namely the attraction of tourists, at this moment in time". Or, as the Mine Captain put it rather more bluntly, "There's not much of the stuff down there, and we want to keep Dunchideock the way it is"."

THERE were, believe it not, people who were taken in by the article, or pretended to be – I was back in that Alice in Wonderland world of mirrors. The telephone rang, endlessly, I was invited to speak at an annual treacle mining luncheon, although the invitation was, mysteriously, not followed up. Perhaps most amusing of all, my old boss, the Field Marshall, said that he had seriously believed me until I described the tunnel in the rectory garden, when he twigged that the whole thing was a hoax. As you and I know, that tunnel – so very interesting – is about the only completely genuine item in the whole story.

I wish that I could show you the pictures that accompanied the piece. One of the great thrills of writing articles is the moment when the proof comes through for checking, and you see for the first time what the Art Editor has come up with by way of illustration. She had excelled herself, finding wonderfully gritty mining pictures, from the 1930s I guess. The whole thing was a hoot.

VIII

January 2007.

OVERHEARD in Cheap Street... Girl with a big bottom, and I guess, a heart to match, speaking in a heightened voice to an old lady, a friend no doubt of her parents: "You going away on holiday this year then?", it was just after New Year's Day. Old lady, supporting herself, as she walked, with one of those three-wheeled shopping baskets: "I suppose so, but I keep thinking about my goldfish!".

One of the joys of journalism is that you develop an ear for dialogue, and, one of the joys of that is that you come to realize how beautifully and simply people can express themselves when unrehearsed and, the irony of it, when they think themselves not overheard. I immediately stopped and, resting it against a plate-glass window, scribbled the exchange down on the back of my shopping list. It was too good to lose – *I keep thinking about my goldfish* – what a world that hints at, what a life it describes, and what a character it suggests. I so sympathise – I keep thinking about my horses, they dominate my every day, and *I* don't like leaving *them*.

Our Christmas holiday was followed by a chaotic interlude. Diana had some long-planned surgery that left her with a foot in plaster, turning me into almost full-time chauffeur/lady's maid. Mind conquering matter she was soon peg-legging it around, directing my labours, but we were both fated to be tied by the ankle for the six weeks it would take for her foot to heal.

Then I, who, unless it be with a broken bone, hardly ever trouble the doctor, was struck with some ghastly bug (picked up in the aircraft?), couldn't ride for a fortnight. It was as much as I could do to keep on top of the horses' minimal routine, bring them across to breakfast in their day-pasture first thing, take them back to the five-acre, Chantry Mead, at lunch-time, give them their tea and 'tuck them up for the night', in the late afternoon.

Getting them across the lane into the paddock in the morning was easy, and a joy really. Like soldiers queuing at the cookhouse, they would always be waiting for me at the gate, Dandy welcoming me with a soft gutteral whicker. I would open the gate, and they takes themselves soberly up the lane, turn into the paddock, and gallop off to their waiting feed-bowls.

Bella, always the most skittish of the two, would often fling her heels up in my general direction, before wheeling round and performing a little dance in front of her breakfast, rather as though she were setting to a partner in an eightsome-reel.

∽∾

LUNCHTIME would see them, bloated from the plentiful paddock grass, fast asleep, Dandy often flat-out, Bella, using the paddock rail as a bar-stool, preventing herself from falling down backwards. Since she broke her knees on the day of the total eclipse all those years ago, she finds it difficult to lie down, or to sleep without falling down, its something to do with the locking mechanism in her knees having failed. She manages, somehow, she's a very happy, healthy horse.

I call to them from the gateway. Dandy will stagger inexpertly to his feet, as though he had never done it in his life before, and, on a good day, they canter across to me. Each seems to think that I will give both of the half-apples in my pocket to the first arrival – I never do, but hope springs eternal in the equine breast, or so it seems, since they both always ask me for the other's share. I lead them back to their night pasture, where they will probably hang around the 'cookhouse door' until tea-time, watching my every move should I happen to be in view, perhaps trundling a wheel-barrow about the garden.

One memorable tea-time, just into the New Year, as I was wheeling the barrow back across the paddock after stacking up the hay-rack, three roe deer belted up the drive, a mother still attended by her now almost fully-grown twins, enormous animals to see, suddenly, close-up, wild, on one's own ground, just by the house.

They were in a panic, lost, bolted from neighbouring cover by who knows what, in blind panic almost. They just saw me at the last moment, the young buck loosing his footing and falling down in his surprise, I can still see where his sharp hooves skinned the turf. They split-up in the stable yard, one opting for the vegetable garden, two for the front lawn – no-one ever knows quite how to approach our back-to-front house – there was no sign of them beyond, or clue as to how they negotiated the orchard with its stout sheep-proof iron fence.

JANUARY was almost half done before I could ride again, then, one morning, as suddenly as it had arrived, whatever bug it was left me. I found myself bringing the horses into the stable again for their breakfast instead of feeding them at grass, and resuming the 'light infantry' pace (140 to the minute), with which I usually get about when out-of-doors.

The relief came only just in time, I was due out with the Vine & Craven Hunt in three days: three days, I reckoned, was just about what I needed to ease myself back into the saddle for a full day's hunting. "You can ride my roan mare, she's a sweetie, the best horse I ever owned" the Master had said when I made contact with the Hunt before Christmas, reminding me of what a dream I live, in my work; I was looking forward to the ride, had thought of it quite often up and down those Verbier slopes.

That first morning back in the saddle I rode Dandy south out of the village up the grandly named Park Lane, in truth a windy, narrow occasionally quite busy road, onto Dungeon Hill. These days some cars come down it as if it were a fairground helter-skelter.

Park Lane is my 'pitch', so I marked where the bits and pieces of Christmas rubbish lay as I rode up, with a view to collecting them on the way home. Dandy, despite being under-exercised and, if anything, over-fed behaved with perfect sobriety, didn't even try to bolt when I gave him a spin up the flank of the hill.

There is a much-used lay-bye at the gateway onto the hill. Along with a broken bale of straw, wheat straw as Dandy soon established, someone had dumped a large trolley thing and several bags of sodden magazines. I'd have to come back with wheels, you can't leave that sort of stuff, it attracts more, and anyway, I'd as soon leave a rotting human corpse in one of our field gateways. Dragging Dandy away from the delicious straw, I set off to walk home, picking up as we went.

If you ever find yourself in North Dorset and you see an elderly gent walking the lanes, his hands full of bulging carrier bags, his horse following, the chances are it's me. Dandy and I have what horse-whisperers call join-up, ie provided there aren't any distractions such as hounds or other horses in the area, he follows me, step for step, just occasionally pausing to browse the verge, but always coming on when I call him. It's one of the reasons why I find it so difficult to think of ever parting with him.

At the bottom of the lane I examined the remains of a deer, a fully grown buck I would guess, which I had seen lying in the hedge just before Christmas, a road casualty I had assumed. It was stripped to the bone now, just a skeleton, but I suddenly realised, in a moment of near horror, how it had met its end. Jumping through the hedge off the road it had trapped itself about the stifle in a stout blackthorn fork: its last hours did not bear thinking about.

By an odd chance it was barely fifty paces from where I had rescued a young deer similarly trapped, between the top strands of a wire fence, some years before. I had heard its piteous, baby cries before I left home one morning, went looking for it: it thanked me for releasing it by nearly lacerating me with its sharp hooves as it kicked free from my grasp. I wonder if it was the same deer – one not very wise or skilled in its jumping?

February 1st.

THE crescent moon that had welcomed us to Switzerland was gibbous by the time we got home, and just a tiny slither when I set off for my day with the Vine and Craven. A long drive to work on such occasions is something I dread – what would happen if the car broke down, the expectant hunt and photographer left waiting – so I had stayed overnight locally with old friends.

It was in a house that Jane Austen knew well, *her* friends the Lloyds lived there, I actually slept in her bedroom. It was amusing, but I guess no coincidence, that the meet next morning was at a place near-by called Wickham. George Wickham, you will remember was Eliza Bennet's rascally admirer, later her brother-in-law, in *Pride and Prejudice*. More than once Jane Austen seems to have used familiar place names for her characters. Wentworth comes immediately to mind, I am sure there are others.

The roan mare, she was a strawberry roan, naturally enough called Jam, was everything that her owner had claimed for her, kind and capable. We had an adventurous morning, and uneventful afternoon, five hours in the saddle, the worst moment being, as usual, dismounting, with one's body moulded into the riding position. One of these days, I know, I shall just collapse into a heap when I hit the ground.

I had promised Horse & Hound the usual fifteen hundred words, cleared with the Hunt, by lunch-time next day, but the article was more-or-less sorted in my head by the time I got home, and, as usual, pure pleasure, a delight really, getting it down on paper. As ever these days, the problem was to convey the flavour of the day without spelling out what actually went on, here's part of it...

"Don't ask me exactly what Duncan and his hounds were up to for the next hour or so, I was too busy getting to know Jam, and trying not to let anyone get in between us and Jam's stable-mate, the handsome grey called Charlie that our Field Master, Jam's owner, was riding, as he led us a breathless dance across and around an estate that was a veritable horseman's paradise. Don't ask me either how many fences we jumped. We'd hardly left the meet before our horses were required to leave the ground: we just didn't stop.

At one stage we emerged from one of the home woods onto the estate drive. There was a broad verge and a gate in front of us, quite a serious gate it looked: "Surely not... hope not...." I thought, and, no, our leader took a left up the drive "... phew!". But, you've guessed it, next time round, I could see from the set of his shoulders that it was a case of straight ahead.

I haven't mentioned the weather have I? The Almighty had been wringing out his smalls since dawn, but he had done the bath towels overnight – you never saw such sloppy ground. Fortunately it wasn't holding stuff, like the Blackmore Vale clay I had left behind me at home, but it was deep, adding not much less than twelve inches to many a takeoff.

That verge was as deep an any of the ground that we were on that day, and how Jam lifted us clear over the gate is a mystery to me, but there seemed nothing that she couldn't cope with. Just four of us made it, small blame to the rest of the field, they were a game lot, hounds weren't running, and there was no call to jump the gate. I would probably have been with them if Jam had not been so determined to tailgate her friend Charlie."

My evasions a fortnight later, with the South Tetcott, in Cornwall, were scarcely less blatant...

"Hounds don't seem to enjoy long meets quite as much as we humans do, and

Paul had quite a job speaking above their clamour as he thanked our hosts, said something which I didn't quite catch about 'trails', and we were off.

Whilst he and his hounds were getting on with whatever they were getting on with, let me tell you about Coriander. She was a 12-year-old bay TB mare, bred by Ptosky for the racecourse where she didn't shine, had done a bit of eventing, and was the Hunt Treasurer's 'treasure'. As well as being Hunt Treasurer, Cori's owner is Pony Club DC, and a Classroom Assistant. It being a Tuesday she had to be in school, unlike several nameless members of the field, and including the youngest whipper-in I have ever seen in a lifetime's hunting, who clearly were bunking off.

I doubt that the feeling was mutual, but I instantly fell in love with Cori. She had a Tom Thumb bit in her mouth, which was slightly worrying, but the breast-plate with its neck-strap was a comforting sight. As soon as I was in the saddle I knew that we suited each other... etc...etc".

.... you get the idea? For all that every hunt I visit does its very best to keep within the law, a modern Hunting Correspondent is reduced to writing about the ride and the weather. How the great Surtees or his contemporary the insufferable 'Nimrod' would have stared: but it's still great fun.

WHEN we had returned from skiing our neighbours were wide-eyed with the news that the whole hunt had come down our drive, "Fifty horses!". We didn't need telling, there was evidence enough on the drive surface. What is more, to get onto our drive they had come down the narrow path than runs from the churchyard under our garden wall. It's the 'way of the dead', barely wide enough for the old hearse that undertakers used to use, which lived for years in our coach-house.

They had had a wonderful day, 'the best of the season'. I was delighted, but less pleased to find that, in squeezing through the wicket off the church path onto our stable yard they had demolished an oak gatepost. I rather hoped, for the honour of my old Hunt, that someone would own up and offer me an apology, but am still waiting. Meanwhile I have replaced it in Ham-stone and brick, keyed-in to the wall, with cement not mortar: it won't be knocked down again in a hurry.

(The honour of the Hunt was in fact redeemed. One of the Masters later confessed to me that he was the culprit, the toe of his boot had fouled the gatepost. He had fully meant to own up and apologise, but in the heat of the chase had clean forgot.)

"The charm of birds".

WHAT do birds say to each other across species: I often wonder? The other day I was struck by the sight of a blackbird and a robin, both cock-birds, perched barely eighteen inches apart on a hedge top, clearly very much aware of and eying each other, oblivious of me. What was passing between them? Insults I guess, and "Keep off!" warnings; it was only the end of January but all the songbirds, as they were daily telling us as well as each other, were actively thinking about nesting.

We know of course that birds heed each other's warnings. Blackbirds and pheasants do 'elf-n-safety' for the whole feathered tribe, brandishing their rattles like demented Air Raid Wardens at the slightest sign of danger. Wrens do their bit too, 'winding their watches' as my mother used to say, and yaffles, green woodpeckers... well they yaffle, set up a terrific row, nothing whatever to do with weather forecasting as some believe, it's more like "Help... lawks a-mercy, here's that beastly man come into my orchard again!" rather than "Wet! Wet! Wet!".

On the morning that I came to think of this, Diana, still hobbling in plaster, was doing her prep school matron bit with the horses when I got back from riding. Thanks to her being out of action and my carelessness in veterinary matters, mud-fever, the curse of us vale-dwellers, has taken hold on Bella's one white sock.

Whilst she was attending to it, my ear and eye were caught by a jackdaw, saying whatever jackdaws say, in the top of one of the two tall trees that stand on the stable yard verge. He appeared to be addressing a small flock of starlings on the next tree, and they seemed rather nonplussed, flying off in ones and twos. What was going on, I would love to have known?

That very afternoon I actually heard a bird say "Tweet-tweet!", which is of course just as it should be. Germans, if you can believe it, think that chiffchaffs say "Zilp-zalp!", which is nonsense, but nothing to what the French think dogs say. The French for "Bow-wow!" I once read somewhere, is "Pan-pan!".

❧

PIDGE was a visitor from some, no doubt distant, loft who seemed to have elected to take a bit of R&R in our garden last summer. He looked like a woodpigeon, but was a bit light in figure, had no ring on his neck, and carried a yellow and green band with black lettering on it on one of his pink legs. He was almost tame, and sat around on the lawn, not really bothering to move much when you went to talk to him. We wondered if he was entirely well, until I saw him preening himself, evidence that he hadn't lost his self-respect so couldn't be that ill.

Jasper, with a friend, Jasper's mother, and their new dog Pippanina, a three-and-a-half legged Dandie Dinmont, were with us at that time for lunch. The children tried a spoonful of ice cream on Pidge, but he wasn't interested. Indeed he flew up onto the roof – the first time we had seen him leave the ground.

Next day a sparrow hawk fled almost from under my feet in the stable yard as I went to get the horses in from grass. I could only hope that Pidge knew what he was about, sitting around in the open. He did in fact survive, was with us for several more days, before disappearing as abruptly as he had arrived.

∽∾∾

ONE evening at about that time another of those instants occurred when birds suddenly burst into your life. We were sitting after supper in my mother's old room where we always sit now, when there was a commotion in the medlar tree outside the window.

A host of blue tits, there must have been a dozen or more, a family I suppose, were flitting about the tree, ever and again darting down to the birdbath below it, drinking, bathing, having a wonderful time, wringing their little heads, shaking their wings like you might shake a wet umbrella. Other birds joined them, a pair or more of great tits, a cock chaffinch, a house sparrow, then, wonder of wonders, a bird I haven't seen in years, a nuthatch. Nuthatches used to nest regularly in the garden.

They went as suddenly as they came. That's the charm of birds is it not? They dart into your life, pay you unexpected visits, then, as instantly disappear, leaving an undying image, an unforgettable, grateful memory.

"Come, come, dispatch; ' tis bootless to exclaim"

"THERE'S a weed in the courtyard that needs pulling up", "Right! I'll deal with it later".... was an exchange at breakfast; then, as I left the house to saddle-up, "You'd better show me that weed, or sure as sin I'll pull up a flower".

The 'weed' turned out the be a rather nice purple creeping thing that was spreading luxuriantly in half-a-dozen places about the kitchen yard, which I had watched prosper, had become rather attached to. But Diana, usually so tender-hearted, was in Red Queen mode; "It has got to go" she said, and that was that.

Home from riding I looked the condemned wretch up in my wild flower book, it was called Self-heal I discovered, as no doubt any proper countryman would have known. I tried the rather propitiatory name on Diana, hoping for a reprieve, but got nowhere. She was adamant, so, like poor Hastings, the offending weeds were bundled off to the bonfire before we sat down to lunch.

I wonder if you have placed the tag that I have quoted above? It comes from *King Richard III*, from a powerful and terrible scene, imprinted for ever on my psyche when we acted it at school. I can still repeat from memory yards of the shortened version of the play we used. It, and much of the other plays, particularly the tragedies and histories, are part of the furniture of my mind, a fact I am ever grateful to my schooling for.

"Woe, woe, for England..." Hastings declaims, when he realises that he is for the block. *"Three times today my foot-cloth horse did stumble, and startled when he looked upon the Tower, as loath to bear me to the slaughter-house".* Powerful stuff, so loaded, and so beautifully expressed. I love 'foot-cloth' for cloth-footed – love it all; where would we be without Shakespeare?

∽∾

"NO, 'e meant ye t'ave it. Ye take it on, bless 'e". I have tried to reproduce the now rare Dorset voice, and you perhaps have guessed that the remark, the very kind remark, was made many years ago. I was trying to return to his widow, a spade that a recently dead neighbour had leant me.

It was not just any old spade, it was what they call a graft, a ditching spade, such as you see in the hands of terriermen. With a long, thin, heavy blade, part crowbar part spade almost, it goes down into any ground with miraculous speed. Beautifully made and balanced, and older even than the long retired farm labourer who lent it to me, it was to become both a treasure and a boast – I have never seen another half as good.

He had spotted me across the paddock hedge digging holes for fence posts and had said "'ere, this is what you need". When I went to return it he said, "No, 'ang onto it, I'll tell 'e when I want 'n", and told me a little of its history, how he had had it all his working life.

There are two angles on this story that are rather difficult to put into words without seeming precious, but I'll try. There is the feeling, almost of comradeship, that an outdoor man has for the implements that share his work and loneliness, and the need in due course to find another home for them, to get them into the right hands.

The reason these thoughts surfaced now is that it is in the nature of outdoor tools to lose themselves. A couple of agonizing months ago I misplaced my graft, I have been almost in mourning for it: yesterday it suddenly turned up.

> *"... when he hath found it, he layeth it on his*
> *shoulders rejoicing. And when he cometh home,*
> *he calleth together his friends and neighbours..."*

THAT'S the parable of the Lost Sheep of course – I think that in fact it must have been a lamb that he laid on his shoulders, unless biblical sheep where very weedy – but isn't that a lovely picture, doesn't it just endure, thanks to those simple words?

Then one reads on; what better evocation can there be of lost-and-found than the Prodigal Son? *"This thy brother was dead, and is alive again; and was lost, and is found".* Surely those words must touch the heart and conscience of even the most hardened stray, I almost weep to read them. What brilliant preaching!

But perhaps my favourite of that group of parables, because it is so shrewdly yet kindly observed, asks "... *what woman having ten pieces of silver, if she lose one piece, doth not light a candle, sweep the house, and seek diligently till she find it?*" This is Diana to a 'T', she cannot rest when something is adrift: if we are due to leave the house – and you must agree with me as to how vitally important it is to be on time, better still early, for all engagements – it is fatal to mention any temporary loss, however trivial, we would never get away.

It had seemed kind not to mention the loss of my precious spade to her. Knowing how I valued it she would have been miserable. So I suffered in silence all those weeks, occasionally asking a neighbour on the quiet if I had by any chance lent it to him.

After finding it at last, I asked Diana in as offhand a manner as I could muster, if she knew where it was. Just as with my lost umbrella, she replied "Yes, it's behind that plank in the garden shed; I hid it there for safety; you'd left it out, I thought someone might make off with it". It had been when I needed the plank to run the barrow up onto the compost heap that I came upon my precious graft.

Putting my finger on the parable of the Lost Piece of Silver was another problem. It is never read in any regular lesson, but it features in my very earliest memories, being read to us children in our pre-war Somerset night nursery at bed-time. I can still see the picture that went with the story, the coin was shown as missing from the woman's head-dress.

At evensong I asked Sister Marjorie, the retired Methodist Minister who lives in the Village and is such a friend to us all. "Luke 15" she said, straight out, without a second's thought, "they are all three there, the lost-and-found parables". And of course they were, and what is more the tape marker in my bible lay at that page; when I took it off the shelf the good book fell open at the very place.

IX

April 26th.

DANDY and I had a job to do on this particular morning, delivering a thank-you letter to the manor house in the next parish: we'd dined there a couple of nights before. I'd drawn a postage stamp with a horse's head on it, on the envelope, as I usually do when I am acting as postman, endorsed the stamp 'Pony Express 0p'.

It's always a problem delivering a letter un-crumpled when you do it on horseback: the thing not to do, though tempting, is to stuff it down the side of your boot. Before now I have had to dismount and actually take my boot off to retrieve it, which rather detracts from the style of the thing if the recipient happens to be watching. This time, not being yet in shirtsleeves, I found a pocket that would accommodate the smart missive, and off we set, Bella, as usual kicking up a fuss at being left behind.

We were unusually early on the road, two enormous school buses passed us as we made our way off Stock Hill, down towards Round Chimneys, where the great Duke of Marlborough spent some of his infancy. We got onto the verge so that they didn't have to check their pace, and I waved them by. Both drivers returned a generous, and I think grateful salute: how one appreciates country manners, and deplores their rare absence!

All the while I was, as ever, keeping an eye out for litter. There wasn't any, the system that I am so proud to have started... works. After Round Chimneys, once a Churchill manor house now a farm, seen across a field to our left, the next historical landmark is a pair of ancient oaks, or rather, what is left of them.

They are actually named on the map, those old trees, Gog and Magog, and are survivors of the ancient Forest of Blackmore, go back to the Norman Conquest almost, when our village got its name. They also mark the southern boundary of what used to be a small island of Somerset, which for some equally ancient reason of land-holding or fealty was marooned in north Dorset. It survived as such until quite recently, tidied up no doubt by some busy bureaucrat.

Just before reaching a house called Somerset Gate I was delighted to see a young Judas Tree well established in the roadside verge. It started life as a seedling in our strawberry bed, and was bought by my neighbour several years ago at the Church Fête. In April Judas trees let the improbable scarlet finery of their exotic bishop-coloured blossom drop, to be replaced in a month or so by equally extravagantly-coloured seed pods: our scion was still half dressed, but looking very healthy, it was the first time I had seen it in flower.

Before turning into the manor's back drive – Dandy and I were in tradesman's mode – we were overtaken by our new egg-man, who lives in the village but runs his poultry on the home farm. I was lucky enough to find him on his feet in the stable yard, and could hand him the letter without dismounting, smiling at the 'stamp', he promised to put in on the kitchen table.

✑

THE ride home was uneventful. But a short stretch of that road is haunted for me by the memory of the day when Daisy, Dandy's dam, fell and broke her knees. I was leading her off Woody, the great hunter I had then, the best horse I ever owned. She tripped, skinned both knees badly, they were like old Gloucester's bleeding eye-sockets in *King Lear*. A grown man shouldn't cry, but I think that I almost wept, I can remember the pain of the sight now – I loved that mare, we had done so much together.

The three of us got home somehow, and the damage, under our vet's care, repaired itself wonderfully, and invisibly, within a few weeks. Almost the worst injury was the burn in my left palm, from the lead-rope being drawn sharply through my hand as Daisy fell. I fancy that I can still trace the scar today.

When Bella broke her knees many years later, on the day of the full eclipse, the injury was far more severe, the scars are still there. Dandy stumbles, increasingly, as I have mentioned. Clumsiness must be in their genes. It was a very foolish thing to do, breeding from far from faultless Daisy: sensibility over-ruled sense but I can't regret it, her progeny have been like driving cogs when I thought life was due to start running down.

May 3rd.

POLLING day again! Hoping that at least one of the Polling Officers would find it amusing I rode Dandy round to the Village Hall. We were in luck, two ladies were in charge, and they were enchanted to have their first vote registered by a horseman. One of them, who instantly fell in love with him, held Dandy whilst I voted.

Dandy, such a tough to ride, is so gentle that I can move him about his box, or make him step backwards, with a word, and the tip of one finger. Surely it is one of the most loveable thing about some horses, that, unless they forget themselves in fright and throw their weight around, they scorn to use their greatly superior strength in the physical dialogue with us humans – it touches on my understanding of the word *gentleman*. Anyway, this lady was quite bewitched by Dandy: I had a job getting him away from her caresses.

Rising Stock Hill, by the Manor House, a man whom I did not recognise was strimming the verge – a contract gardener I guess. Seeing us, he switched off his machine and stepped up out of the road, supposing, wrongly that the noise would have upset Dandy, who is bomb-proof. So I put him into a canter, waving my thanks as we passed, and getting a broad smile and an answering wave. I know that I have said it before, and recently, but how one appreciates true, generous, country manners!

∽◇◇

IT HAD been quite difficult getting Dandy, solo, out of the box he must now learn to share with his sister. I was determined to do it single-handed, and had given the matter some prior thought, but Bella did her very best to burst past me in the wake of her brother, before I could fix the breast-chain in the doorway. When, having hitched Dandy, I went back to shut the door on her she was furious. Her enraged trumpeting followed us down the drive.

Dandy started trumpeting too as we turned off the road into Park, the field above the Manor. He never normally calls for his sister, but boxing them together seems to have strengthened the bond between them.

Coming down off Dungeon there was what looked like a rather fat roe grazing below us. This turned into two deer, and then three, as they sep-arated and set off up the hill at my approach, stopping every now and then to look back at us. They were, I suppose, a mother with last year's twins.

And then, further on, a large hare lolloped out of Broad Alders, and, I could hardly believe my eyes, or my luck, it joined four others, which were playing what looked like ring-a-ring-a-roses on the steep hillside. They made off at the sight of us too, but pausing every now-and-then briefly to resume their game.

"It's a bit of paradise up there" Diana said to me, when I told her of it – my very thought.

∽◇◇

TURNING into Stonylongs off the road, a welcoming party of ewes and lambs galloped bleating towards us – usually they run away, I don't know what or whom they took us for. The lambs were barely a week old – more of paradise really. A small gang of heifers, newly on that pasture and not yet settled, formed up like a troop of cavalry ready to charge. I did what I always do when cattle shape up like that, turned Dandy and walked steadily towards them. They slunk off: cows are usually easily cowed I've found, so long as you don't have a dog with you, but I wouldn't try it with a bull.

Bella was in a high state of excitement when we got back, had sweated up a little. It was a relief to have got that first essay in a new routine safely behind us. She led out with just a rope loose round her neck as usual when I took her join her brother in the paddock. She's a gentle creature too, but,

– 85 –

typically, she greeted Dandy with a playful bite before they wandered off to graze.

May 5th.

GREAT excitements! As we drove home late from a dinner party early this morning, entering the village, Diana saw a big blaze out west in the direction of Hay Wood. A police car, lights flashing, roared aggressively up the narrow lane towards us, hardly giving me time to crowd the hedge to make way for it, wondering the while how many 'units of alcohol' were in my system.

Though the wind was against it, there was an undeniable bonfire smell in the air when we got home. It was still evident when we got up at the end of a short night – we both assumed, as one does, that it was the smell of cigarette smoke on our clothes that one always brings home from dinner parties, then we both suddenly remembered the blaze. Diana went off to Badminton Horse trials: I saddled Bella and rode out to find evidence or news of the fire.

The dinner party had also brought news of a quite different sort. We heard for the first time of the death of someone who had been the biggest man in farming hereabouts through much of my lifetime. He had been like a local chieftain, you might say, when in his prime. I remembered him well as a rising, brightest of bright young men, who lent my father a horse to hunt when we first settled here.

Stanley was past ninety, very recently, tragically, had had to quit home for a 'home': you couldn't wish he had lived longer, but it was the end of an epoch for those of us who have known this neighbourhood post-war. So, as well as looking for the seat of last night's blaze, Bella and I were carrying a letter of condolence to the farmhouse up on the flank of Dungeon Hill, where I first remember him living, and where one of his son's lives now.

PARK Lane was at its best as we rose the hill, red campion, stitchwort, and much else that I cannot name, taking on from the bluebells up the banks on either side; a feast of sun and colour, it's a simply lovely place. When we reached White House Farm, I fell in with Karen, who was on a racehorse, cooling it down for its jockey after fast work on the hill: I usually meet Karen driving a tractor. She said "What fire?" when I asked her about the mystery blaze.

We rode along together the few paces until I could drop off the letter and turn homeward, but soon struck across the fields for Hay Wood. The smell of burning was in the air again when we got under the wood, but there was absolutely no sign of the seat of the fire, nor could I find anyone in my various rambles that day that knew anything of it.

Hay Wood's bluebell carpet was just beginning to fade, with wild garlic, or ramson as my book tells me I ought to call it, taking over, and here and there my favourite spring flower, yellow archangel. In the thick of the wood Bella suddenly became alarmed, and alarming – I think that a roe buck had probably got up behind us.

It is not amusing being on a plunging, frightened horse in close cover, and you realise why French huntsmen wear tall boots that envelope and protect the knee. But she soon settled, and we rode quietly home, none the wiser about the fire, or the speeding police car. It must be just a matter of time before word of it comes in, this is a country village after all: I shall just wait and see.

∽∾

WE didn't have to wait long. My report of a mysterious fire and speeding police car soon ran round the village, bringing a neighbour to our door. He had known Hay Wood since boyhood, knew every inch of it, had gone, twice, walked the wood looking for the disaster site, and found nothing. Was it possible, he tactfully asked, that Diana had mistaken the light of the setting moon, seen through the trees, for a conflagration. Had it been a particularly good dinner party, was his unspoken question?

The moon was indeed at full, seeming to be especially large in this eclipse year, and due to set in the late dawn: it had been a good dinner party: a local farm had a big bonfire on the go, accounting for the smell: the police car was, evidently speeding to some emergency other that our forest fire which was, well…. all moonshine.

> "Horatio - … but this is wondrous strange!
> Hamlet - And therefore as a stranger give it welcome.
> There are more things in heaven and earth, Horatio,
> Than are dreamt of in your philosophy."

I HAVE always supposed that this kindly rebuke of his friend by Hamlet, was intended by Shakespeare for all of us – we should try to be open-minded about things we do not understand.

I am going to test your open-mindedness now by telling you that when I left the house this morning and went to unlock the church, it dawned on me, with ridiculous certainty, that the horses would not be waiting for me at the gate of their field, as they have been this last month, but that they would be at its very far distant end.

Sure enough, they had their bottoms against the hedge, backs to the road, the best part of a quarter of a mile away, and did not stir a hoof until I had walked every pace of it. Worse, Dandy sauntered off disinterested when I collared Bella: as usual, he wandered back to be caught when he heard her chewing on what I had for her in my pocket.

How did I 'know' that the horses would change their habitual behaviour on this particular morning? Search me! All I can tell you is that that is what happened, and it is not the first time, I quite often seem to receive small inconsequential messages from them.

Once, as I have told before, coming home from midnight mass on Christmas Eve, I felt driven to do something I never normally do, disturb the horses after 'lights out' – I hate to get them unnecessarily to their feet, hoping for an extra feed, when they might be lying down and asleep.

Bella was 'cast', lying helpless on her back, having rolled into the foot of the wall of her loose-box: a night spent like that could have been the end of her. How did I 'know' that something was amiss in the stables: you tell me? I am as sceptical as Horatio about ghosts, need to see one to believe in them, but life has taught me to play my occasional hunches.

May 7th.

I WAS confidently expecting to find the horses by the gate this morning, but they were, as yesterday, as far off as five acres allow – so much for that psychic hunch! They seemed to know what I had in mind however, as, seeing me, they trotted briskly up, and I let them take themselves the short distance down the lane to turn into the paddock where their breakfast was ready for them.

It is a hands-off routine that they appreciate and I treasure, dating from a couple of years ago when I was for some months 'crippled' by a fall, but today is its last. You have perhaps been wondering why I have been accustoming Dandy and Bella to share the same, very large, loose-box? It is because we have bought a pony, for Diana, he arrives tomorrow.

In anticipation it feels like a change of life, I cannot but selfishly (and secretly) mourn, the three of us, my two horses and I, have been such a happy, handy triangle. Time was we had as many as six horses about the place, but for some years now it has just been Dandy, Bella and me. How will Harvey fit in, it's a big worry?

Harvey is a 14.1 tri-coloured gelding, 13 years old, with a great reputation and a price to match. All our local gang of course will want to know what we paid for him, but we're not telling: all I will tell you, is that it was more than my father paid for this house. His full name Harvey Wallbanger, which is perhaps not the happiest name, since his only acknowledged fault is not liking being left in a stable on his own. We shall see.

Diana fell instantly in love with his advertisement in *Horse & Hound*, I liked him on sight, and because he voluntarily nuzzled me when I went to stand close to his head, he felt right. Also, I have a weakness for coloured horses, having never known a bad one.

Ever since we clinched the deal Diana's carefree certainty about Harvey has evaporated, it's "I do hope this…" and "I do hope that…". For my part, who am not given to having second thoughts, I just long to have the little chap here, get on his back, get him settled in his new home and in mutual charity with his new companions. Until then it must be a very anxious time.

∽∾

ONE of the things to be done in preparation was, as I have mentioned, to accustom Dandy and Bella to share his box. It's a good six paces by four, quite large enough in theory for two horses that are on good terms with each other: and so it proved. I fitted a second manger diagonally across from Dandy's, and gave some thought as to how I would juggle them in together single-handed. Bella had nipped in once or twice before unofficially, visiting the boys' dormitory naughty thing, but I wasn't sure how either of them would take it as a regular arrangement. It turned out to be a case of "Hey Presto, no problems!", they liked the new regime.

I just had to invigilate their first breakfast, manhandle Bella away from her brother's manger a few times, like trying to put a pushy lamb onto another teat. But they soon settled: they love it in fact. No doubt Bella misses being able to reach the light switch (such a bore when one is saddling up in winter and she plunges the place into darkness – you could almost hear her giggles), but, apart from that you never saw two happier horses. The sight of them looking out over the door-chain together warms my heart, and makes me almost optimistic about the arrival of the gooseberry.

May 8th.

I FELT as if I were both condemned man and executioner going out this morning to saddle Dandy. I hate playing God with animals, suddenly visiting chaos on them, turning their settled lives upside-down, without warning stealing away their precious security. Why do we always end up betraying the creatures that share our lives, depend on us and trust us?

I was to ride Dandy and lead Bella, get them both some exercise before Harvey should arrive. It is something I have not done for a year or so, not since Bella learnt how to break away from me whenever I attempted to go across the fields and she felt delicious grass under her feet.

It was early, not yet 8am, and we headed in an unusual direction, west to Blue Town, where the road to the village leaves the main Sherborne-Dorchester highroad. The name, that of a small outlying settlement where half-a-dozen families live, is not recorded on any map, nor have I ever seen it written down, it's just part of local oral history, I delight to record it here.

Somehow getting into the saddle without a hitch – forgive the pun, there was no ready means or securing Bella whilst I mounted in the lane – we trotted blithely off through the waking houses, Bella almost silent on her unshod feet. It is three years since we left off shoeing her: it's been a great success, Duffy checks her feet regularly, they keep hard and healthy. She can go almost anywhere in comfort now, except on flints.

Home within the hour, with a heavy heart I turned them away on some fresh grass in the far division of Chantry Mead to start Day One of our new life.

⤌◦⤍

WHILST waiting for Harvey to arrive I did what I have done before in unhappy or unsettled intervals, weeded the gravel whilst keeping an eye cocked down the drive. It came back strongly to me that that was how I had killed time during the final hour of Perdita's life, waiting for the vet to come, she the while sunning herself on the lawn all unconscious that she was approaching the final moment of her long, happy life. Perdie was our last dog, an adorable and irreplaceable lurcher.

Bella evidently knew something was up. Why wouldn't she, horses don't have to rely just on our poor five senses? Instead of hoovering up the fresh grass that I had left her on as a special distraction and treat, she watched my every move over the quite distant fence.

All too soon a vehicle appeared, its ramp was down, and Harvey entered our lives; winning, confiding, gentle, pony-like. With his late owners, we led him out to his new home, the meadow he is to share with Dandy and Bella over a tall, live, electric fence. He put his head down to graze – no fireworks, no fandango, nothing… it was a non-event. Phew!

⤌◦⤍

NO DOUBT it was foolish of me not to let him settle, but I determined to ride him within the hour, to break the ice, and get the introduction over. We were both a bit apprehensive as I tacked him up, and there was a little trouble getting him alongside the mounting block – he was shy of me. But, once in the saddle, surely the safest place to be with anything except an unbroken youngster or a rogue. He was a dream of quiet composure, and off we trotted.

"I wouldn't canter him first time out" Diana had cautioned, but he seemed so biddable that, instead of turning for home at the top of Park Lane as I had meant to, I turned into Shells, the big field that wraps round the west flank of Dungeon. The ground at the foot of the field is like poached concrete, the weather having switched moods so rapidly at the change of seasons that quite a lot of winter pasture has seen neither harrow nor roller, is deeply pitted and rutted, very treacherous to ride.

Higher up I knew it to be smoother, but as we gained the top a violent squall hit us; I would have seen it coming had I been less attentive to my mount. We might have been at sea it was so sudden, in a moment we were soaked, Harvey almost blown off his feet. We tacked downhill into the lee of the wood, where, just a day or so before, that group of hares had been sunning themselves at play.

No cantering this time, but Harvey had stood a much sterner test. He seemed a very steady little horse, and, off his back a couple of times on the way home, to pick up rubbish, I realised what an advantage 14 hands has over 16 at that game. He's really no smaller than the ponies I used to play polo off.... I wonder...? Silly thought... much too old.... forget it.

The peace in Chantry Mead proved to be short-lived. Bella having taken a great fancy to Harvey, went into season, and behaved quite shamelessly, all spoony over the high electric fence. Dandy took serious umbrage, and looked dangerous. The virtuous triangle formed by me and my two horses seems to have been replaced by a vicious one, one mare and two geldings. Will they ever settle down into a happy *ménage à trois:* not if what the experts tell us is correct? What next: must I get myself another mare?

May 9th.

RODE Harvey down to Dark's Bridge before catching the London train to start on a new project, researching the history of the Queen's Body Guard, for a book I am to write in time for their 500th anniversary, in 2009. The bridge is not a sinister place at all, despite its name, I once saw a kingfisher there, it darted, electric blue, under the bridge, illuminating the moment unforgettably the way birds do. The stream, un-named, wanders off to join the Caundle Brook, on the way feeding the Churchills' old weir and fishpond at Round Chimneys.

You won't find the name Dark locally today, but the 1851 census shows six of them resident here, a washerwoman, a labourer, and four children. The name suggests, dare I write it, that they were dusky travellers who settled for a time in the bridge-side spinney, perhaps she used the stream for her laundry, and he had some hand in building the bridge.

That census shows the population of the village being then twice what it is today. There must be the remains of deserted dwellings in all sorts of corners. I plan to go and explore that spinney. Though tiny, it is called, rather grandly, Sandclose Islands, a name that tells you that it was enclosed and is on greensand, a good spot to squat. How I would love to know all about the Darks!

On the way home we picked up a 'Top Man' plastic bag with an empty vodka bottle in it that had been thrown down in the verge. Now there's something truly 'dark': what sad, bad, sorry secret lies behind that empty bottle thrown down so fecklessly in a country lane? (It was just as well we picked it up, 'the council' cut the grass verges next day, we would have had broken glass and white plastic strewn everywhere.)

"… when a man is tired of London, he is tired of life;
for there is in London all that life can afford."

I GOT the impression that I was virtually the only Englishman in London when I eventually got there, I was certainly the only man I saw wearing a hat. I had sought advice from an expert on whether or not I needed to wear a bowler for St James's Palace, "No" he had said, "just your gent's natty suiting", sharing an old regimental joke at some city tailor's expense.

The last time I wore my bowler to London I got the feeling that people were gathering in knots, giggling, and pointing at it. I did actually hear an old Indian gentleman saying to his daughter, as we passed each other on an escalator, "That's how English gentlemen used to dress in the old days!". It was one of the most acceptable compliments I have ever been paid. That was in May, when we went up for the State Opening of Parliament: it was just as well that I was properly dressed on that occasion, as I have told you.

As always, I found the noise in London crushing, I can't take it for long. It's an inhuman place; you would think that man had been set on this planet for no other purpose than to make a hideous, painful din. It was to be such a blessed contrast to wake up next morning to total silence, broken only by the insistent chattering song of a chaffinch outside the bedroom window. The same bird flew up through the orchard ahead of me when I went to unlock the church, perching on the garden wall, and then on various tombstones, to repeat its song.

I got lost finding my way into the Palace. Security is of course strict, "Bring a photo ID, and the policeman on the barrier will let you in" I had been instructed, but I had forgotten where the barrier, the entrance to the maze, was. Luckily a cleaning lady, going off duty, took pity on me, and admitted me without question (another unlooked for compliment) to a central courtyard, where I got lost again. Such signs as there were, were alarming rather than helpful, on parking lots marked as "Reserved for Prince Harry, Prince William" and so on, but I was clearly getting warm.

I could hear the distant sound of a military band; then, close at hand another congenial sound, the clip-clop of hooves. An immaculate brougham drawn by a beautifully matched pair of bays entered, somebody important-looking delivered something to a door marked The Marshal of the Diplomatic Corps, and I realised for the first time in my life why ambassadors are said to be accredited to the 'Court of St James' – I was standing in it, more-or-less, what an adventure!

A small sign said 'Reception'. I rang, it was York House, whatever that may be, and another kind soul directed me through an archway in the royal labyrinth. I was at last at the right door, and took the first step on a new and rather alarming path.

May 15th.

SANDCLOSE Islands turned out to be a magic place when I went back on foot to explore it. No more than quarter of an acre, if that, its old trees no doubt knew all about the Dark family, supposing I am right in my supposition that they camped in the central clearing there, old Mother Dark, as I imagine her, scrubbing away by the stream, her man tramping off daily at dawn to work the land or mind beasts for a local farmer, or building his eponymous bridge.

There was a handful of old oaks, outnumbered by sycamore and ash, some of which had evidently grown up from stumps – a habit that produces such strong, interesting second-generation trees with multiple trunks. Dark no doubt had a hand in felling them, the cordwood providing firing for his wife's boiler.

But there, I was daydreaming! There was no sign whatever, apart from the suggestive name of the bridge and the entry in the census, that anyone ever lived there. A footbridge, a single plank with a rickety handrail connecting two of the islands, told that it was still, today, on somebody's occasional route, although it is not on any public footpath. The only other sign of life, apart from birdsong, were badger snuffle-holes.

As I say, it is a dreamy, magic place, islands of beauty and stillness in a world gone ugly-mad; I mean to know more about it, unlock some of its secrets.

"Words, words, words."

MOST of us, I notice, have quite irrational but almost violent dislikes of certain words and phrases, I know that I do. I think that it is a function of loving our quite unique and precious language, and indignation when we hear or see it, as we judge, misused.

Some people seem to use English as if they were deaf to the meaning of the words they are using, blind to the images those words give rise to, and do so without any suggestion of self-irony. How else can you explain, for instance, the way spokesmen and commentators employ that moronic oxymoron 'friendly fire' to describe perhaps the most poignant and tragic of battlefield accidents. 'Own goal' would be better, though hardly appropriate to the context, but at least it is not mealy-mouthed. Think of having "Killed by Friendly Fire" on your father's, son's or brother's gravestone, or on the village War Memorial!

Soldiers, and I mean squaddies, have a great way of coining their own punchy words and blunt epigrams to help round off the rough corners of their tough lives. I cannot at the moment call any to mind that are fit for this page, let alone fit to be repeated in the brave new world of political correctness, but some of them glint like jewels in my memories of the tank-park, barrack room and field.

"M' knee's f....d Ma'm", one of my troopers reportedly said to the Regimental Medical Officer, the wife of one of our officers, on sick parade one morning – such a gorgeous combination of soldier's argot, brevity and courtesy. I really warm to people who say what they mean in a few short words: the opposite makes me feel almost murderous.

X

MY strongest memory of a lost summer is standing with Dandy in the field shelter, marooned there by sudden torrential rain. I had him saddled, ready for a morning ride, our last outing together for many weeks, when down it came, and went on and on, as though it never meant to stop. We were enduring the wettest June and July in memory: it had played havoc with farming, and put paid to my beloved polo club – they just could not get on the ground to play.

Dandy is so companionable, so endearingly trusting, when in confidential mood, his velvet muzzle pressed up against my hand, one large, so expressive eye, engaging mine. He stands like a rock, breathing softly, but just every now and then shuffling a few inches nearer, as though he really values my company.

There is a statue of a cavalry trooper with his horse in the Royal Scots Dragoon Guards museum in Edinburgh Castle which exactly catches what I am trying to describe, that almost numinous thing between man and mount which would take horses, against every instinct, into danger, steady them, when wounded even, when surrounded by hellish din and bloody horror, so long as they feel that trusted presence in the saddle, and a familiar, calming hand upon the rein.

September 10th – 16th.

"For this relief much thanks:..."

A WEEK spent in Milan was almost literally 'what the doctor ordered'. "You are not to do any lifting, and certainly not get on a horse for six weeks" the surgeon said. He was a delightful Pole, a horseman, who shared my admiration for his country's Trakehner breed, had three of them at home he told me.

I had taken this admonition with a pinch of salt, it was after all his job to be cautious, and there were soon sixty or so bales of hay to get in. But when I got home, and surreptitiously – Diana was in league with the doctors – removed the dressing, I discovered that what I had thought was to be keyhole surgery seemed to have been done with a tin-opener. You would think that I had had a Caesarean (Equal Opportunities?), except that there was nothing to show for it but a letter-box scar: it was evidently a mistake opting for a general anaesthetic, I should have kept an eye on what was going on.

What is more, my horsy friend had told me that the plan was to put some surgical gauze in there, to help hold things together, but it felt as if he had used a bit of chicken-wire: it still smarts, fully a month later, as I write this. Discomfort and snail's pace were evidently to be my lot for as long as it took: a week spent *en flâneur* in Milan seemed quite timely.

Diana's injury was if anything worse, and more frustrating, as it threat-ened to put her off-games, both tennis and riding, indefinitely. Like her pony, as I shall tell you in a minute, she had injured a tendon, in her instep, and she did it, almost to the day, when at last the vet gave Harvey the 'all clear'.

HARVEY'S arrival had indeed, as I had feared, turned our settled life upside-down and inside-out. It wasn't just that he needed separate, minimal grazing, this being as bad a year as I can remember for ponies, whose access to rich grass must be rigorously restricted for fear of their developing laminitis – the crippling and very painful affliction of their feet that haunts all pony owners when grass is rich and abundant.

He had to brought into the stable for eight hours or so daily, and with a chaperone. All the grazing had to be divided up with electric fencing, and, so that all three could have a share of fly-free shade, the shelter even had to be partitioned into 'his' and 'theirs'.

What is more, it was very disconcerting that one's wife, of a certain age, seemed to have re-joined the Pony Club: any day almost I expected her to sport plaits or a pony-tail. You never saw such fondling and cosseting, such imagining of ailments, such a collection of remedies, special feeds and dietary supplements – the saddle-room shelf looks like a tart's dress-ing table (I imagine), with all the bottles and packets of this and that.

Harvey wasn't surnamed Wallbanger for nothing, as we were to learn the hard way. One morning, not much more than a week after his arrival, just as we were shaking down into some sort of manageable routine, Diana was due to catch a train to London. We went out early to bring all three in, she still in her night things. Harvey must have been handy to the gate, as she got him to the stable whilst I was still fifty paces or so behind, leading in Bella and Dandy.

When she shut the stable door on him he went completely wild – liter-ally went up the wall, actually getting one hoof over the eight-foot high box partition. It must have been a terrifying performance. Hearing her screams I dropped Bella, and ran in with Dandy.

Harvey calmed immediately, but the damage was done. A sonic scan disclosed that he had tweaked a suspensory ligament; six weeks total rest, preferably box-rest was prescribed. Disaster! You can see why Milan beckoned so strongly.

"DO YOU really need *both* these sandals?", I asked Diana, as I tried to cram her overflow into my already heavily pregnant case; and, as we leave, "We are three minutes early, does it matter?". Thus my skittish attempts to lighten the horror of departure for Bristol airport, long before dawn, and one of the nastiest drives I know, up the A37 past Shepton Mallet, limping north in a queue of spastic elephants. Getting away is always hell.

But by lunchtime we were with Louise and her children. By the cocktail hour I was where I had longed these last frantic weeks to be, sheltered from the strong evening sun at a pavement table, a glass in front of me, taking in a scene that is so completely different from home that it spells both heaven and holiday for me.

∽∾

WHAT did our short break consist of? For me, each morning, as soon as I could establish that I would not be missed, heading for the cathedral square, the *Piazza del Duomo*. If I call the cathedral the Duomo, please don't think I am being precious, like calling Paris 'Paree', it is how I think of it, that magnificent, cavernous, lovely place. It is inseparable in my mind from a magic turn-of-the-century-Christmas, when it snowed, a cardinal preached, the acre-ous nave was crammed with a pious congregation, and I heard the towering organ playing Handel, full blast.

Next stop a favourite table in a favourite café in the Galleria Vittorio Emannuele II, an arcade of giant proportions where you could garage a whole fleet of double-decker buses two abreast, that runs north from the *Piazza del Duomo* to the *Piazza della Scala*, and a building I hope one day to see the inside of, Milan's historic opera house.

There, at a pavement table, I would sit and watch, and listen, as the world rushed by, fixing my eye and my imagination momentarily on each hurrying figure. To each one its story, each one seen for a few seconds of its long trajectory from the cradle to the grave. I just love people-watching, guessing their stories.

Two police appear stage left, tall in their white helmets, imposing – Italian bobbies have not been turned into boobies, PC PCs, as so many of ours sadly have been; ill-led as they are, demoralized by the modern political ethos, and constantly wrong-footed. Milanese police look 'fell', as if they mean business, but approachable, and are impeccably smart, proud of their appearance, he the best part of seven feet top-to-toe, she, with raven hair down her back, a good foot or so shorter. As I watch, she raises a finger at a cyclist, who immediately, smilingly, dismounts – you are of course not allowed to bicycle in the Galleria.

They exemplify, those two constables, something that I believe that I see, and that I admire, in Milanese. They carry themselves well, almost as though on stage, almost as though performing, are in command of themselves, know their worth, will stand no nonsense, yet they are the most friendly, perfectly mannered people that you could hope to meet.

You don't see scruffy Milanese, swaying beer-bellies or hippo-bums, let alone cowled, skulking, foul-mouthed, shuffling youths who are patently at war with themselves, poor things, and with civility. We call it self-respect (never to be confused with self esteem): Italians call it *bella figura*.

∽∾

A GREAT excitement one morning was taking the children to school. All three, Sophia aged six, and her twin siblings, two years younger, are bi-lingual, and go to the *Collegio San Carlo*, a short walk from their home in the *Via Boccaccio*.

It was the first day of a new term, you never heard such a din, nor saw so great a scrum. Every child and parent in full cry, the building, with its marble walls and open stairwells designed, one would think, purposely to amplify the noise. The young mothers, each one, not least Louise, dressed to be admired if not to kill, were a delight to see as they swooped to greet each other and embrace.

Collecting time, mid-day, was if anything more overwhelming, a cross it seemed between redeeming a winning ticket on the favourite at the TOTE, and rush hour, underground, in Tokyo. Such fun, such theatre, and it happens twice a day, the whole school year round.

Since I am for ever rabbiting on about how I hate London and its noise, I have perhaps some explaining to do as to why I love Milan, where there is seldom a silent moment round the clock, why I think of it almost as a second home. In truth, I can't explain it, except by saying that Italian noise amuses me, it's a performance to be enjoyed, not an ordeal to be endured: I find that I can laugh at it, it's theirs not ours, like other people's children, parents, dogs. Above all, I don't have to take it back to Dorset with me.

∽∾

BAD news from home came to disturb our peace of mind on each of our first two nights. Bella's leg was 'up'… again; the neighbour who kindly baby-sits our horses had had to inject her. Bella has developed a chronic malfunction of the lymph glands, leaving her at the mercy of any slight infection; it is a painful condition, incurable. Although I can hardly bear the thought of it, it will be the end of her if it persists.

Don't laugh at me, but I prayed for her in the Duomo, and in another church that I visited, next morning. I believe in the power of prayer, if only as an antidote for helplessness: I don't seriously suppose that the Almighty can take an interest in Bella's off-hind leg.

Then, much worse, news of another outbreak of foot and mouth disease, in Surrey, linked to an earlier one, supposed safely contained and over. What agony for farming, a stop again to hunting, a shadow over the coming season and my planned tour in Scotland and the Borders.

We came home however to find nothing worse waiting for us than a mouse drowned in the sump in the cellar floor, one courgette doing its best to be a marrow, and all the rest of the garden complaining loudly of neglect. I couldn't get out fast enough to see the horses: Bella's leg was....

'...neither up nor down'.

"The fault, dear Brutus...."

BEFORE we left for Italy I had found myself at a loose end in the dentist's waiting room, ridiculously early, as usual, looking for something to read. All that was on offer were magazines about motor-cars and football, which I suppose someone must read or they wouldn't publish them.... and women's stuff, amongst which, in a publication called 'Red' I found a picture of a horse, and rather a nice article by a girl who explained that riding kept her sane. "Hear, hear!", I thought regretfully, before turning the page and coming across the month's horoscopes: "Stars, what September has in store for you".

As I have mentioned, I have no time at all for superstition of any sort. So long as one watches magpies carefully and avoids walking under ladders such fears are just for the feeble-minded. Similarly, astrology seems total rubbish to me. How can it possibly be that one twelfth of the world's population, from bushman to banker, zoologist to Zulu, can be subject the same specific threat or promise in any given month?

However, just out of curiosity I did read *"PISCES – The Sun watches over your working life, so, when it eclipses on the 11th, you feel the impact on your career. Stable situations crumble* (Harvey??) *and new conditions present themselves almost daily, but Pluto's forward thrust from the 8th suggests that, actually everything is going to your advantage. Keep a low profile and hang on until the dust settles".* "Well, that's alright then" I thought, surreptitiously filleting the magazine and pocketing the page.

The 11th was when I found myself sitting in the Galleria, feeling on top of the world. But I did just wonder, re-reading that guilty page, if I had been wise to write a cheeky letter to one of my Editors just before leaving home. Those great men, Editors, do not always have their sense of humour readily at hand.

He in fact sent me the kindest of rejoinders, and I found on my screen on getting home a delightful writing commission from an entirely unexpected quarter. Presumably, bushmen, Zulus, bankers etc were contemporaneously having pleasant surprises "as the dust settled" all over the world. Nice thought!

"... is not in our stars but in ourselves...".

September 20th.

"BE careful when you go round blind corners... I'm thinking of you, not just of Harvey" Diana called down the stairs as I set off to take her pony for his constitutional. Though neither of us can ride yet, we walk him daily, for fear of his taking harm in his feet from overeating and total idleness.

As Harvey and I turn out of Locks Lane into what the Electoral Roll humorously calls our High Street, over my shoulder I catch a glimpse of the usual clutch of mothers and children waiting at the War Memorial for the school buses, which I would not like to meet, we hurry on. Always beautifully driven, the buses almost fill the road, especially now, before the hedges have been trimmed. The tarmac surface, as I have not seen before, is stained with squashed blackberries – surely the hedge-fruit never normally falls before somebody picks, or something eats it?

We are heading south out of the village with a brisk wind in our faces, the first time it has come round from the north in weeks. The outline of Dungeon Hill is up ahead of us; how I long to be up there, mounted. Just a few days more now, I shall ride Bella first, the others are unshod, she doesn't need shoes, and she's the kindest ride anyway.

We beat the busses, turn into Stonylongs, and I let Harvey graze a bit of my neighbour's grass, leaning back, my elbows on the top bar of the wicket gate. It's one of the most restful standing positions that I know, and brings back a memory of the fist time I hunted Bella, on St Valentine's day, a dozen years or so ago.

On the way home she had spooked at the canter, I fell from her, rather violently, on my head, passed out. I just remember heaving myself up onto a gate in that position, seeing her galloping off into an endless vista of grass meadow, reins flying; and then came-to, in the saddle, half way home, a busy main road, somehow crossed, behind us. It sounds improbably, but happens to be true, and it tells you something, I'm not entirely sure what, about horse and man and what goes on between them.

I can hear Bella yelling for Harvey as we get close to home: he seems indifferent, content for the moment with my company. That tells you something, surely, too; we know all too well, with two enormous vet's bills to show for it, how he goes mad if left for so much as five seconds on his own.

Molly, the wolfhound, meets us as we re-enter Locks Lane, next her naughty kennel-mate Jack, surname Russell, then Stitch the family cat, and finally their owner, Sue, who so kindly looks after the horses whilst we are away. "There's a free fireworks display here this afternoon", I tell her, explaining our plan to make a first nervous attempt, whilst they have no shoes on, at running the three horses in the same field together. "They'll be alright, after an initial sort-out", she says, echoing my most optimistic thoughts. Let's hope: we'll see.

"Lady behave!..."

... I say hopefully to Bella, as I lead her out from the stables to join the two boys, who at last seem to have settled down peacefully together. Sue was right, there were no fireworks, the most difficult thing was catching Harvey, to put him with the others. Clearly he sensed our nervousness. Since the day of his arrival I have never had the least difficulty catching him, but this afternoon the Devil seemed to have got into him, and it affected Dandy too. Only faithful Bella came, as always, to be caught.

I took her, jibbing, and complaining bitterly, into the stables as bait. It worked, Harvey came to hand, and when I turned him away with Dandy nothing much really happened. They charged around a bit, Harvey rolled a couple of times, Dandy occasionally close-circled him, which I guess is stallion behaviour, but neither gelding went to savage the other as we had so feared.

After an anxious half-an-hour or so they settled down unconcernedly grazing, and took Bella's return very calmly. For her part, having flirted brazenly with Harvey over the fence since the day he arrived, she didn't seem to want to know him. No question of "Together at last!", she repulsed him with heels and squeals, although she was yet again in season. Why she should behave thus was a mystery to me, but Diana seemed to understand it, and, as to Bella coming into season, said that she was just faking it.

Dandy's behaviour was equally if not more incomprehensible. After a bit, he snuck up behind Harvey, started grooming his back-end, his gaskin, hamstring area and hock, giving it a good nibble, Harvey grazing unconcernedly the while.

Again, Diana had the answer, "It's submission", she said. What on earth was my sixteen-plus hand hunter doing submitting to her fourteen hand pony: my fear had been that Dandy would chase Harvey over the hedge? I begin to think that I know nothing whatever about horses.

Not caring to leave them completely un-invigilated, I got a bucket and started picking blackberries, consciously turning my back on them, whom an hour before I would have happily sent to the kennels – I can't stand horses that won't be caught, it's such an unappealing way to carry on.

When Woody, my late great Irish hunter, was with us there wouldn't have been a single berry in reach to pick, he had a taste for them, and could stretch up the best part of ten feet. After a short while I heard movement behind me, all three horses had come the length of five acres to see was I was doing, with a view to joining in. Then a nudge in my back from Bella as good as said "How about me?".

Soon I was feeding the odd blackberry to each of them: all friends again. Later, over a mug of tea, Diana said "Why don't we have a short ride together tomorrow, my foot seems much easier, and you should be OK now?". It was such a happy, happy day!

September 25th.

"… lays its eggs inside a paper bag…".

WOKE trying not to sneeze, for fear of waking Diana. I needn't worry really, she sleeps like a babe in the early hours, lucky thing: I have to try to bridle my mind from going wandering. All too often it takes me on tip-toes upstairs to work, it's my best time of day. We are the original owl and skylark, Diana and I.

It was a big day coming up. Diana was to take herself in to Dorchester to see the Consultant, and find out if her foot has really healed itself – I shan't let her play tennis until we are 100% certain – I am to ride Dandy for the first time in six weeks.

"Don't do anything silly (bother!), you are not to canter him (Damn!… was planning to nip quickly over Dungeon), remember he's no more fit for fast work than you are (nonsense… elf-n-safety!), and he's got no hind shoes on (true)". Feeling bolshie, but as ever obedient, I went to juggle the horses, Bella and Harvey, who are an 'item', to be left on the lean day-grazing, and Dandy to come in for saddling. It sounds easy, but is in fact quite a struggle, as they are all three of them mad for the split apples that I always have about me; it's an amazing year in the orchard.

When I have picked out his feet and tacked him up Dandy declines to approach the mounting block. As if he were seeing it for the first time, he just doesn't trust the old doormat that Diana filched from where it kept my feet insulted from the stone floor in my workshop and put down, weeks ago, on the cobbles in the stable doorway, to save Harvey's tender, girly, unshod feet. It is just one of the many 'special arrangements' that his whirlwind eruption amongst us has brought about.

I speak harshly to Dandy, tell him not to be WET! As usual that does the trick, but he leaps away from the block just as soon as I am in the saddle, almost before. He's in a naughty mood evidently, by token of which, instead of his usual sluggard crawl when leaving the stable, he walks out beautifully down the drive, we're off!

❦

BEFORE going to get Dandy I had checked the sheep in the orchard. One of Neil's 'barren' ewes, who have spent the summer eating down our spare grass, dropped a couple of lambs on the day after our return from Italy, and there are evidently more on the way. He had warned us in advance, had meant to take them away, but then the Foot & Mouth movement restriction prevented him.

I like having lambs about the place. This is an attractive family, they nestle cosily in the sunny angle of a buttress that my father and I built to stop the orchard wall tumbling down, when we first came here, over half a century ago. It pleases me a lot, as it would have pleased him, to see our work put to use in this way.

I would not have thought of riding over Dungeon had not the wireless told me that morning that the movement restrictions had been eased. Soon comes another sign of this welcome, if slight, relaxation of the throttle-hold on farming, an enormous cattle lorry rattles by. Dandy doesn't turn a hair, nothing of that sort worries him.

Who does not feel for farmers, our farmers? As well as Foot & Mouth they have Blue Tongue Disease now to fear, it is spread by midges we're told, not to mention endemic Red Tape Disease, spread by men in suits with ball-point pens and clip-boards.

Plan B, as I may not now ride over Dungeon, is to inspect a strange corpse lying in the grass verge on Stock Hill, above the Manor. We spotted it yesterday when riding the other two horses; Diana thought it was a cat, but I was pretty sure that I had seen feathers. Sure enough, it was a large, quite a large, bird, its identity, as seen from the saddle as clear almost as it was improbable: I rode on, meaning to take a closer look on the way home.

Silliness of any sort being off the agenda I just rode tamely down towards Dark's Bridge, saving Dandy's bare hind-feet on the generous verge – it's a very old road, which, until it was metalled, evidently wandered a bit between equally ancient hedges. Such a blessing it is where they didn't close-corset roads when the land either side was enclosed two centuries ago: Stock Hill Lane is like a droveway almost, and well treed, such a precious place.

Our progress was arrested by the sight of a beer can, rendered razor-sharp and lethal on account of it being sliced in half when the verge was mown. I get off and turn for home. Stock Hill is not my pitch, and it wasn't in bad order, but 'zero tolerance' is the name of the game if you fuss about litter. I have a bag half full of the stuff by the time we get back to the mysterious casualty.

I pick it up by its bill, it is neither a duck nor, since it has a barb on its long rapacious beak, a small heron, nor is it any bird that we ever see round here. It is, improbably, what I at first sight took it to be, I fling it to where it can rot down, or feed other creatures, out of sight. How on earth did a dead cormorant get to be there?

∽⬝⬝⇌

SNEEZING seems such an odd thing: do other animals do it, not seriously as we do, I believe? I fancy that I have seen a cat sneeze, but only slightly, it would be quite an inconvenience to a hunter, death to its prey – surely mice don't sneeze, except in Beatrix Potter's stories. Or do they? Horses snort, endlessly, but I don't ever recall hearing one sneeze. An elephant sneezing doesn't bear thinking about, and one can't imagine birds or reptiles sneezing, a crocodile for instance.

For humans it can be more than an inconvenience. I'd have to read the book through again to be certain, but I seem to remember that it was a sneeze that betrayed Jim Hawkins to the pirates, when he was eavesdropping on them in *Treasure Island*. How involuntary is sneezing, do courtiers on duty do it, have you ever seen a sentry sneeze, or a parson sneeze in church, I don't ever myself recall needing to sneeze on parade? Can you really stop a sneeze, as I was told once, by making a Hitler moustache with a finger pressed on your upper lip: it didn't work for me this morning?

And what about the pleasure of sneezing, at least for the sneezer, the snuff habit that came from Mexico and was so strong in Europe in the 18th century, leaving us all those lovely snuff-boxes? It seems rather odd, not to say uncouth, today. Do people still take snuff, I have an idea that they do, and it is not that long since the fashion died. Did not one's grandmother's grandmother take snuff?

Sneezing has its language and its culture too. *"Gesundheit!"* Germans exclaim if you sneeze in their presence. I thought, until this moment, that it was just an onomatopoeia, rather a good one, but my dictionary tells me that it is a noun, for some comic reason feminine, and means 'health or soundness', the equivalent of our exclamation "Goodness!" perhaps.

We say "Bless you", perhaps once-upon-a time really meaning it, seriously, since sneezing could be a symptom of the plague, as we are reminded in the final line of *Ring-a-ring o' Roses*, before we all fall down. You can't even blow your nose in public in Japan without causing raised eyebrows my son Miles tells me, sneezing must be almost a capital offence. And what are we to make of the American expression, "not to be sneezed at"?

If this has been no more than a parade of ignorance, please forgive me, it all started at about 5 o'clock this morning. Diana is back, with good news and bad news, and a neighbour has just rung to say that 'our' sheep are all out in the lane...

I RUSH out of the house, crook in hand, and check first in the orchard; mother and babies are there, she looking a bit anxious. No sign of the other ewes, and, yes, they have pushed through a gate onto the lawn that has not been opened in years and I had neglected to fasten. They are in the drive, looking full of mischief. The fishmonger in his van appears fortuitously, pushes them up to me, and I turn them into the paddock, panic over.

And Diana's news? The Consultant is evidently on my side, she is to be very careful until her foot is scanned in two months' time, tennis is out, but she may ride, gently. I shall be extremely firm with her.

DUFFY came that afternoon to check all the horses' feet, as he had done just before we left for Italy, and advise on how long we might go on gently working them unshod. We had the usual Dutch auction when it came to paying him for the two sessions. "How much for a visit?" I ask, cheque-book in hand. He names a ridiculous figure, I quadruple it and smuggle the cheque unseen into the front seat of his van. Thus country life and old soldiers carry on.

I had been milking him for funny stories, having been once again ensnared into agreeing to give an after-dinner speech. Duffy's stories are usually not for mixed company, certainly not for *Guardian* readers, but one of them might just do for my Scottish audience. It's more than a month off, but I already dread it.

"Didn't the horses behave well this afternoon?" Diana said over tea. Indeed they had. There had been no problem catching them, and they came in and went out together like lambs, and, except for Bella, always the prima donna, were pictures of obedient, quiet patience under Duffy's inspection. It really seems as if Hurricane Harvey has at last blown itself out.

XI

September 27th.

"It all makes work for the working man to do"

I FIND myself getting quite attached to Harvey, the interloper. If the black on his face gives him a slightly satanic look, and he has a bit of devil in him, he is companionable, and, like most equines, does what he is told if you are firm with him, and he understands what is wanted: voice usually does it. Diana is off to Castle Carey for the day, so I walk him out, taking care of his mimsy feet where there is loose gravel lying about the road.

Two fine trees mark the southern edge of the village, as we retrace our steps of a day or so ago. On the right an enormous oak leans across the road, as if holding an umbrella over passing traffic. It's a pollard, as most old oaks are, 'girt', the trunk cut through at about twelve feet from the ground centuries ago, but allowed to grow out massive limbs when they ceased regularly harvesting fencing timber from it, with the advent of iron wire.

Then, across the road, a few paces on, our great ash, another pollard, stands as a waymark over the old stile, where the public footpath used to enter our land. I say 'used to', because a year or so ago somebody in County Hall with nothing better to do with his time and our money, insisted on boring a hole in our hedge and putting a duplicate stile in, forty paces down the road.

The result of this paper-driven nonsense is that ramblers must now walk the road for those few unnecessary paces, round a blind corner, rather than simply cross it, as users of the old path had done, on their way to church no doubt, since before that ash tree ever grew to mark the path's route and the location of the stile.

The map had a minute, no doubt post-luncheon, error on it: to the bureaucratic mind one cannot argue with paper, whatever an ancient tree, an old stile, the obvious direct line of a path, local knowledge and common sense might otherwise suggest.

HARVEY exercised, I extract Dandy from the besieging, beseeching trio, all after the apples they can smell in my pocket, saddle him, and off we set… but he seems lame, at least somehow ever so slightly awkward in his gait as I lead him away to mount.

We had noticed it, we thought, in the field, in the evening after we had run the three horses together for the first time: had he perhaps wricked his shoulder in the fracas? Then it had seemed only momentary, had rapidly passed off, as it did now. By the time I have got him through the gate into Lady Mead and onto Brook Furlong (don't you just love those old field names?) he is trotting sound.

A fox cub pops up ahead of us as we enter Great Wootton Wood, occasionally turning to inspect us, its ears erect, and then we are on Dungeon again, at last.

In Park Lane I dismount and lead him, for the usual reason, picking up as we go. Matching my pace with his I can tell that, at the walk, he is indeed favouring his off fore, the smaller of his ill-matched front feet, just as he did when the vet looked at him last year. Later, he's actually trotting lame.

Certainly no more hunting for him; and *Horse & Hound* are just now on to me for my ideas for the coming season... when and if it comes. I'll borrow of course when I travel, but when hounds meet here... I wonder if, at a pinch, Harvey...? Whatever happens, I mean to keep Dandy as long as he is enjoying life, and then take him on that terrible sad journey to the kennels, as I did with his mother.

WE nearly came to grief in Park Lane. Something coming down the hill behind us frightened Dandy, he tried to bolt, almost knocked me off my feet with his full hurrying weight. I just managed to keep upright, and maintain my hold on the reins – I had a single finger hooked through their buckle, leading him at full length, negligently I will admit.

You couldn't blame Dandy. How often do you see a flying saucer in a Dorset lane? His bulging backwards-looking eye had spotted, bowling down behind us out of the blinding sun as it cleared the shoulder of the hill, what looked like an enormous hat. In fact it was a three-wheeled bubble-car, low and skimming silently along the road, my neighbour's latest toy. We exchanged greetings, he apologised, needlessly – I'm much too casual on the public road, as Diana is for ever telling me – and the moment passed.

Home, and Neil trundles up the drive in a small truck. He's allowed to move his sheep up to 1.87 miles (three 'kilometres'), and he's taking them home.

I don't know a more pleasing sight than a man working his dog with sheep. Tea, short for Tia Maria, a black and white collie so prompt, so on her toes, so quick in mind and body, so eager to please, so delighted in her work, yet so tactful, commanding without frightening the little flock: is there a happier creature on God's earth that a working sheepdog? In a matter of minutes, babies and all, they are loaded, and that's the end of sheep for another season: I shall miss them, I like having sheep about the place.

September 29th.

"His name was Harden, James Harden, he was
a captain in the Light Dragoons".

WATCHING a re-run of the BBC version of *Bleak House* last night I was reminded what a happy thing, film, and then TV adaptations of classic novels have been in my lifetime. One forgets the minority of bad ones: the good ones stay with you, send you back with renewed appetite to the books.

All of us who worship Jane Austen must be grateful for the fillip that recent screen revivals of her work have given to the readership of that retired, short-lived, spinster, who 'spoke' so quietly, but to such effect, in a different world, all those years ago. It's a welcome paradox, the triumph of worth in a vapid age: how I wish that she could speak to us today about 'celebrity'.

Great Expectations was the first of such adaptations that ever I saw. It was before I had read the book, so I carried into the reading of it John Mills as the adult Pip, Jean Simmons as Estella, Francis L Sullivan unforgettably as Jaggers the lawyer, and so on. This is a reversal of the usual thing, when one finds that the screen version of a familiar novel has some of the characters 'wrong', ie quite different from the picture in one's head: it's often the same when one first stumbles on an illustrated edition of some book loved since childhood, in which you have long ago made up your mind as to what the characters look like.

Usually the feeling of irritation soon wears off and is replaced by enchantment, although I cannot say that I have ever seen an entirely convincing Lizzy Bennet or Anne Elliot. But how often has one not lived from week to week dying for to the next episode of, for instance, *The Forsyte Saga*, *The Mill on the Floss*, or *The Mayor of Casterbridge?*

The Brontës, Trollope and Thackeray have come across very well too, and no doubt other authors whom I have forgotten. Film and TV are just made for costume drama, bringing those old times and scenes alive, and if there are small mistakes in the period detail it is great fun spotting them.

It amazes me for instance that some directors and producers, not to mention actors, do not seem to know that the first action of any gentleman on meeting a member of the opposite sex, then as now, is to bare his head. Pinching the brim of the hat between the thumb and forefinger, with a self-satisfied smile, is all very well for a Belgian private detective (I am a Poirot addict), but it would never have done in the cathedral close at Barchester, let alone in Highbury. Table manners on the screen are also often anachronistic, one does not, and Jane Austen's contemporaries certainly never did, speak with a mouth full.

One cannot cavil at the film actors who do not look at home on a horse, or at the palpably modern bits in their horses' mouths, but I do wish directors could resist making horses stand on their hind legs and whinny. Rearing is, fortunately as rare as it is dangerous, if you will forgive the pun.

Bleak House was wonderfully done, so powerful the drama, so brilliantly cast, so beautifully realized in dress, location and scenery, it was absolutely gripping, and fun, a faultless piece of television, with Gillian Anderson's Lady Dedlock an unforgettable *tour de force*.

Dare I say that I think that it was better than the book: who am I to criticise the great man? It is just that I prefer authors who manage to beguile us with real characters, especially real women, in believable situations. Dickens is for me a wonderful entertainer and storyteller, but the writers that I most admire work in less vivid, more everyday colours.

September 30th.

"Mother of the free."

SINCE last night I have been wrestling with a problem, trying to fit words together along the following lines...
Land of Health and Safety...
... a second line eludes me, must give it some thought... watch this space.

What sparked the endeavour was the band concert we attended in Sherborne. A Light Infantry Territorial Army band, up from Exeter, was performing in aid of The Army Benevolent Fund. It was a simply lovely treat to hear all those old tunes, the buglers, and especially the 'Evening Hymn and Sunset', when, as the Bandmaster said, "We think of all those in uniform who have fallen, serving their country".

But before the magic ever got started some poor apologetic chap was obliged to get up on the stage and give us a brief elf-n-safety lecture on where the fire exits were. As if the Digby Hall was on the point of taking off to fly the Atlantic, we couldn't read the perfectly clear signs anyway, and as if a gathering of old soldiers and their wives needed to be nurse-maided, treated like a lot of children. "What next..." I wondered, "seat-belts, in case we fall to the floor?".

How I loathe that sort of thing, how it takes away from the style of an occasion, reminding us, as if we needed to be reminded, that we groan under a tyranny of small-minded, otiose, overpaid, feather-bedded, humourless and second-rate officialdom!

THE news from Chantry Mead is that Bella has gone back to Dandy, leaving poor Harvey always a few paces off, as if his breath smelt, and making horrible faces at him when I lead them in together. What a tartar that little mare is!

Dandy is definitely lame in the shoulder. Yesterday, Sammy from the Old Forge came to help me saddle up, she wants to learn about horses. I got her to trot Dandy up to me; there is no mistaking it, no grounds whatever for hoping or pretending otherwise. So that's six weeks at least off for him now: when ever will we get our string sorted out?

Everywhere, everything, was incredibly still as Diana and I tip-toed on eight bare feet out of a sleeping village. All curtains drawn, no traffic, and, as we rose Stock Hill, not a sound or breath of air, no-one and nothing astir in the whole of North Dorset it seemed.

Being the fifth Sunday of the month it's a Benefice service, for all seven parishes, to be held at Caundle Marsh. I know that it means yet another brand under the cauldron when I get to hell, but I am just not benefice-minded. It's our parish, our beautiful little church for me, and then only when they use the Prayer Book, and there is a fair chance that the lessons will be read from King James's incomparable Bible.

I coax Diana off the road for the first time, onto Park, the field above the Manor. It's a start. She is so nervous for Harvey's feet that she more often than not dismounts and leads him when we are on the road, and so nervous for his leg that we just walk round Park. It's step in the right direction: he is to have his shoes back on next week, so I hope that we will be able to do more after that than just tamely potter.

∽≫≪

I HAD had another mishap coming down Park Lane yesterday. Bella told me, the way horses do, that there was a horse following us down the road. I stopped in a gateway, asked the rider if she minded company, and was joined by a horse that I 'recognised' and a jockey whom I 'knew'.

Having worked on this assumption for a minute of so of rather one-sided conversation, it came to me that my companion was looking a touch blank and puzzled. I studied her horse more closely, and her, and then asked the poor girl outright who she was. She was not my farming neighbour's daughter, but someone I had never met in my life before, riding a horse that I hadn't previously set eyes on.

Maybe my mind was on other things, it often is these days. Glanvilles Wootton on an Autumn Sunday morning might be a picture of silence and tranquillity, but the world seems to be in such a mess. Louise had rung in from Italy that morning, asking after her step-brother. "Is Miles alright? The papers here are full of that Japanese photo-journalist killed on the streets in Rangoon, horrible pictures. They say that he was with Associated Press?".

Panic! I 'signal' Miles, *"Are you in Burma, was that one of your team they killed, are you OK? D"*. His reassuring answer, received today, has him safe, he got no further than Bangkok, *"The plan was to go to Burma, but they're not giving visas"*. *"Bless them!"* I thought: I doubt anybody else anywhere in the world is invoking blessings on the Burmese military junta.

October 1st.

DIRTY weather was blowing up this morning as Bella and I topped Dungeon, great grey clouds crowding across the vale and from Bulbarrow on a strong cold north-easterly wind, with already a bit of spit in it. We were glad enough to slip into the lee of the hill as we turned for home.

Crossing Little Alders, one of the Manor fields, I noticed, not for the first time, how strikingly a herd of cattle makes just one narrow path across a field, as if they were negotiating a minefield not flat open pasture, following each other exactly, sharp hoof after sharp hoof, cutting the turf precisely, you would think almost that it had been done by a machine. Sheep do it too, and so of course did man, when he first entered on this virgin country, unconsciously laying out today's network of roads and tracks. It must be an instinct, to follow in the footprints of your own kind.

It was pouring by the time we got home, and, since no-one was there to tell me not to, for the first time ever, I rode Bella straight into narrow aisle between the two looseboxes so that at least the saddle could come off her back dry. Harvey was waiting anxiously for his 'ex' at the gate, and got a frown for his pains, Dandy was sensibly keeping his ground in the field-shelter.

I didn't just get soaked, as so often when riding, a problem in my head un-knotted itself. What do you think of this....

> *"Land of Elf-n-Safety,*
> *Bur-eau-cra-a-acy,*
> *Ri-i-isk assessments*
> *and Diversity.*
> *Wider still and wider..."*

... the rest of the words fit the sense perfectly without alteration. I'm rather proud of it, must get to work on a politically correct *Jerusalem* now.... here's the first line...

> *"Did sandaled feet, in ancient time...?"*

... the sandal of course being the modern equivalent of the jackboot; proud badge of the *Guardian* reader, master of us all and pioneer of the 'great indoors'. You don't see many sandaled feet up on Dungeon Hill.

October 2nd.

"DON'T look too closely at our horses, they're filthy", I warned the newspaper man, who delivered as we set off for an early ride on what promised to be a busy day. "I got on one of those things once.... it moved. So I got off!", he replied, echoing a distrust of horses that so many country people have, not least some of my near neighbours, men who have perhaps spent a working live, possibly handling farm stock, outdoors.

There's nothing so catching as nervousness, and no domesticated creature is more nervous than a horse: it is unsurprising that people who have not learned to trust horses are afraid of them, the feeling is no doubt mutual. Of all improbable things, they think they are going to be kicked. I have spent my life mucking about with horses, and never once been kicked.

I have been trodden on, by mistake, quite often, and usually by my own fault; been nipped frequently, in play, nipping being part of horses' small talk; bitten in anger, quite sharply, twice that I remember, again due to my own tactlessness or inattention, but never kicked. Never intentionally, seriously hurt. On the contrary, I find horses to be the gentlest, most confiding of creatures, selflessly discounting their own great strength, true gentlemen.

Once home from our ride, I cast an anxious eye down the drive, hoping not to see a small corpse outside our nearest neighbour's, Mrs Ross's, gate. Delivering the 'paper late last night, in the pitch dark, leaving her gateway, I had tripped on something, nearly fell. Thinking it was a bit of tree, we've had a lot of storm damage recently, I bent down to retrieve it: it wasn't there. Supposing I had kicked it away, I felt for it round about with my crook, located it, bent down again... it had prickles.

Diana was touchingly concerned for the health of Mrs Tiggywinkle when I told her, not a jot for me: "Had I trodden on her etc?"! Evidently we both survived the stumble: the drive was empty.

October 7th.

"Under the greenwood tree..."

WAS Thomas Hardy ever in this house? It is not impossible, but perhaps, if one takes a magnifying glass to the dates, not really likely. Our church was 'restored', my father would have said 'ruined', in 1875/76. The architect was G.R.Crickmay, Thomas Hardy, almost right up to that time, his assistant, was employed, as we know, and as he later regretted, on church restoration. That was how he met his first wife, Emma, a tragic figure, when he was sent by Crickmay to work on a church in Cornwall.

That Thomas Hardy *did* work on our church is locally spoken of and believed, but I have an uneasy feeling that I started that hare running, if it is a hare, myself. I just can't remember if it is something someone once told me, or something I thought up for myself when I began to take an interest in him at school.

Parson Woodman senior was at that time coming towards the end of his long rectorship here, before handing over to his son. It must be a grand-daughter of his, Eva, whose height at the age of twelve in June of 1875, along with those of her brother Cyril and of her sister Fay, is recorded in pencil behind the shutter in the girls' bedroom, one floor below me as I write. Surely I may be allowed to believe that the Rector kept in close touch with the work going on in his church, and in all probability invited the young architect's assistant in for a cup of tea?

The difficulty is that in 1875, aged 35, the year after he married, Hardy's life was on the cusp, between Dorset and London, obscurity and fame. On balance, I have to admit that the great man probably never stood in our church, or saw the rooms that mean so very much to me. I would love to be corrected.

✁

WHAT sparked these thoughts was recently reading Claire Tomalin's brilliant biography of Thomas Hardy: she almost makes me like the man. Certainly I have learned from her to credit him with being a dutiful son, a kindly brother, and being fond of and liked by children. That goes a long way towards his rehabilitation!

What I don't like about him is the contradiction between the qualities he seems to promote in his characters, and asks us to admire, and his own way of carrying on. Like so many anti-hunting 'bunny-huggers' he could be perfectly foul in his treatment of his fellow humans. I call it 'artistic deficit'.

How often has one not read a panegyric of some dead giant, the obituary ending with a throwaway line that as good as says "Oh! By the way, he cheated on his wife"? Why should genius have licence to behave unkindly? I don't buy it. Give me Jane Austen or Elizabeth Gaskell every time, they truly teach us how to live.

Walking Harvey back across Stonylongs this morning, the church in view, the bells suddenly started. I thought with compassion of our Church Warden, whose husband's 60th birthday party last night – 400 guests or more on their farm – must have kept her up until the small hours, supposing even that she got to bed.

We had been playing bridge, in aid of the Cattistock Hunt, at Melbury, seat of the family with which Thomas Hardy's mother was in service. Home just before midnight, Diana insisted on dragging her reluctant husband to the birthday revels, made him take to the dance floor, and 'Twist again, as we did last Summer' etc. But at least we got to spend some time in bed.

Somebody, I never worked out who, no doubt one of my father's old patients momentarily trapped in an alcohol-induced time-warp, said "Good night Doctor!" as we left. I never cease to wonder at the indelible mark my father left on this place.

It is the first Sunday of the month, the Children's Service, always extremely well attended. Young blood runs strong in this parish, as witness the congregation at our Harvest Festival last Friday, and the crowded Village Hall for supper afterwards, the children delighting us and themselves as auctioneer's runners when all the produce from the church was sold off.

But my heart is with the days when every service was a children's service, I cannot but regret the well-intentioned 'restoration' of our liturgy. One of the things we lost when our church was done over all those years ago was a musician's gallery. Those who remember Thomas Hardy's happiest novel 'Under the Greenwood Tree' will enjoy the *irony* of that – to use, I hope rarely in this book, a much overused and misapplied word. It was a time when modern-minded clergy were taking a new broom to old, cherished practices. Look where it got them!

∞∞

AS WE left the village later that morning, heading westward for Blue Town, crossing Osehill Green, Diana would have us re-visit the scene of last night's revels – 'Hog Roast, Music and Dancing, 8pm 'til Late'. Osehill Green is, by the way, another of those old names, like Blue Town, that survive orally; can you grow osiers on a hill, one thinks of the Somerset Levels as being the sort of place that osiers prefer; perhaps someone famously in the past kept geese there?

We were heading for Castle Cary, where I am still required as odd-job man, re-hanging Melanie's pictures now that she has moved a few doors down South Street in that lovely, congenial small Somerset town,

For some reason Diana wanted to examine last night's marquee. Should I be smelling a rat, does this tie-in in some way with the growing stock of champagne in our cellar? No doubt I will be told when I need to know?

All the local farming neighbours, men and boys, women and children, had turned out to help clear up, and were thoroughly enjoying a second, impromptu party. It was a reminder of how close-knit, and how inter-dependant the wider farming family in a rural area is, and a subject worthy still of Thomas Hardy's pen.

∞∞

EMMA Hardy, as I have mentioned, comes across as a tragic figure. There is a picture of her in middle age that I had never seen before, in Claire Tomalin's book. Although it was almost painful to look at, I found myself turning to it again and again, as the story of their marriage unfolded. I have seldom seen a photograph that could speak so poignantly; yet it eludes description.

They had an idyllic courtship, and happy early marriage, but then, no doubt through faults on both sides, it fell into misery and mutual torture, or so it reads to me. When she died, guilt, and memories of former happiness, overwhelmed him, and he wrote what is held to be some of his best poetry. I give him no marks at all for that, any more than did his second wife.

As Tom, my father's old gardener/groom, who remembered him well from his Bockhampton childhood, used to say " 'e had nothing to say to the likes o' we". There was a hardness about him that I can only forget when I get lost in the wonders of his stories.

My Hardy shelf tells a story of a very different marriage. The volumes all come from the Macmillan Pocket edition, first published in the early part of the last century, and, mostly bound in lovely soft maroon Morocco. Starting when they were first engaged in 1938, and running through to 1952, my parents gave them, 'with love', to each other, the fly leafs recording where in their holiday travels, and when, the gifts were made.

For years I was puzzled by the following inscription in the flyleaf of 'A Pair of Blue Eyes'...

"Gracie with love from Alan, Lilliput, Dorset, Sep'28."

... where on earth, I wondered, could Lilliput be? A recent news story locates it near Poole.

October 15th.

"Now, Esperance! Percy! And set on."

"HE'S adorable, this little horse" Diana said, slipping to the ground from the saddle, to lead Harvey up the drive in case a stray bit of loose gravel on the tarmac should bruise his mimsey-pimsey, big girl's blouse feet. He's now shod in front, hind shoes on next week, but no sign yet of him being released from cotton-wool and bubble-wrap.

I too have come really to like Harvey. It's a good start that he seems to like me, but I like the way he stands where I put him, when I'm tacking him up. Bella wanders vaguely off if you don't tether her, and often does so when you do. She quite understands the purpose of the quick-release highwayman's hitch, just as she has mastered electric light switches.

We'd had a rather sad adventure on our short ride. The herd of Jerseys in Park, the field above the Manor, were all gathered resting in a far corner with just one single beast slowly plodding the length of the field to join them. As we passed her, she turned to retrace her steps, as though anxious at our going into the quarter of the meadow she had just quit.

She had a full milk-bag. Diana said, "Go quietly, she's got a calf somewhere". Sure enough, a very large, very dead, calf lay where she had come from. She stood over it lowing a couple of times, then, as we left, plodded off again dejectedly to rejoin the herd. We wasted no time, you may be sure, in passing on the news to the Manor.

IT WAS only a *short* ride because I was engaged to test-ride my neighbour Robert's great horse Percy. I am sort of half thinking of offering to buy Percy, and Robert is sort of half thinking he might sell him to me, although he is, very wisely, nervous of disposing of a horse next-door. Hunting is starting up again. This is Monday. I have a plan in my head to take Percy to look at hounds when they meet in the village on Saturday, for *Horse & Hound*: Robert doesn't know this yet, nor do *Horse & Hound*, or the hunt in question.

I call Percy a 'great' horse because he won the Members' flat race at our point-to-point; I took a shine to him then. He's a very fine-looking big grey, clean bred, 11 years old. Possibly too much of a horse for an old man like me, he certainly looked a handful when the start was delayed at the point-to-point, and there might be a problem with his brakes. The only satisfactory way to find out is to ride him out with hounds, and why not earn a bit of money doing it? After filling a pocket with quartered apples I walked round to Church Farm to make his better acquaintance.

He was friendly enough, I've no interest in horses that don't like humans. I made up to him, asked him "Is this the start of something big?". But he was very odd about the apples. I've never met this before. Instead of gratefully grabbing the quarter apple, and flicking it back with his tongue to be dealt with by his molars, and then immediately asking for another, he just nibbled it daintily in my palm, before ingested it. Had Percy never previously met an apple, it hardly seemed credible?

I saddled him up, under Lyn, the groom's, eye, getting in a fearful muddle with the breastplate, a bit of kit I haven't used in years. Julia's chickens were clucking and foraging round Percy's feet and mine, and suddenly a cock crew, thrice, almost under his belly, a beautiful bird, a Lavender Arakana Julia later told me. No-one apart from me took the least bit of notice, I jumped a mile. Then off we walked to the mounting block, and what might just be the start of a big adventure.... my new hunter?

PERCY strode off admirably, I liked the feel of him: I know that I have said it before, but horses are just like regiments and individual soldiers, you know immediately if they are any good. As we entered on Stonylongs he showed me that he thoroughly understood gates, and, once on the road, that normal traffic had no terrors for him. Lyn was in charge: the plan was to do a bit of fast work on Dungeon Hill.

"Take care he doesn't try to make off with you when we get through the gate onto the hill", she warned. He didn't, he just took an honest hold as we cantered up the flank of the hill, trying to accelerate away whenever he heard Omar's drumming feet get close, as any self-respecting horse would, but I felt that I was in charge. Omar is Julia's Arab sport-horse.

A surprise awaited us on the summit of Dungeon. Standing on the top of the iron-age rampart, staring down at us from all of ten feet up as though about to charge through the intervening bushes and wire fence, was the biggest, whitest, ghostliest steer you ever saw.

Percy turned like a polo-pony, and made as if to bolt down the way that we had come. It was a useful test, if a bit scary and unsettling. He took no more than three paces before answering to the bit and coming to, and he settled, quite quickly, after what had evidently been a genuine fright.

Home after a good hour's ride, with no more adventures, it had been a promising start. Robert was there when we got back to Church Farm. He readily agreed to my plan for Saturday: that just leaves one Editor and one MFH to be squared.

WHEN I was tacking up Bella and Harvey earlier that morning the initials 'IA' had suddenly occurred unbidden to my mind. It was a flashback, I think, to a drama that Jasper and I had had in the same situation, when we were tacking up, prior to my riding out with his mother, on the previous day.

Bella had taken fright from some distant movement in the manor ground, over our boundary hedge. She had thrown her full weight back, suddenly, proving the use of the highwayman's hitch, as I was able to release her from the terret before she could trash her head-collar. Harvey took fright too. Suddenly I had two strong animals doing their best to break away from me, as though I were playing two enormous fish, and none but a small boy to assist me.

The 'Immediate Action' required was to open the stable doors and get the two frightened and excited quads safely shut in their loose-boxes. With Jasper's prompt help peace was soon restored. I taught him how to tie a highwayman's hitch later that morning over lunch.

It was at Sandhurst that I first encountered the notion of IA. If you are operating a weapon in battle and it runs out of ammunition or jams, nothing is more important than to do the right thing quickly to get it firing again. As cadets on Weapon Training we had the relevant IAs endlessly drilled into us.

I have no doubt that IAs have saved a few of my then comrades' lives, although I forgot them as soon as I left the place, never handled a weapon again if I could possibly avoid it. I'm not very good with guns, and, like my father and my eldest son, never have liked sudden noises.

But the useful notion of Immediate Action has, as you can see, stayed with me. Army officers, especially cavalry officers, may affect to be 'laid back', but in fact there is small place for sluggishness in any proper soldiering, little use for the 'pending tray' and 'the back burner'.

At the Regular Commissions Board at Westbury, where I spent the last few years of my service, deciding each week who out of a batch of schoolboys or schoolgirls might or might not suit Sandhurst and a career in the Army. We used an excellent interview and selection technique, little changed since I myself as a schoolboy went through it. A 'Sense of Urgency' was one of the essential criteria we looked for and graded candidates by.

If I have failed to remember any of the IAs we learnt at Sandhurst I have at least carried in my head all these years a saying learnt there, so useful to a soldier... "It's later than you think!".

October 17th.

"Tu-whit, tu-who – a merry note..."

A TAWNY owl was wittering on, endlessly repeating itself in the desultory but insistent way owls do, at dawn this morning when I woke. It was a pleasant reminder of where I was... blessedly at home. Yesterday we travelled the breadth of the country, by rail, to attend a family funeral in Essex. Trawling the east end of London, where so many people live cram-jammed together, I could not but think of riding on Dungeon Hill, of all those sad wild fatherless boys whose murderous antics we read about almost daily in the 'papers, of how lucky I have been, and how unfair life is.

Returning, we switched to the underground at Stratford, it was high rush-hour. You wouldn't transport animals the way we were crowded into that train, there seemed to be limbs and body-parts at all angles, filling every space. It was like some ghastly Dali or Picasso nightmare picture come to life, I don't know how humans bear it.

I felt quite low in spirits when we got home, and went disconsolately to bed. It had been a long, necessarily sad and rather stressful day, not helped by my own incompetence, ie finding the car almost out of petrol as we made an early start with a train to catch. More than that, I was oppressed by the reminder of how most of the world lives, betrayed by a crass ideology, poor schooling, a gutless church, cancerous bureaucracy, and nerveless polity (have I missed anything out?).

"That England, that was wont to conquer others,
Hath made a shameful conquest of itself".

TRAVELLING up to London that morning, at each stop our carriage had recruited groups of crop-haired men of military bearing, ribbing each other, but soberly dressed. They seemed to be retired generals mostly, all on their way to a memorial service for one of their number untimely dead, at St Margaret's Westminster.

As they filed out at Waterloo, one, wearing a familiar tie, leaned toward me, saying quietly as he passed, "All safe back, yesterday!". Now a retired Lieutenant General and the Colonel of my old regiment, he had served under me, commanded a squadron for me, many years ago, just as I had commanded our regiment during his warrior father's colonelcy. So the strong, precious, inimitable family thread of the regimental story runs... may it never break! The Light Dragoons are back from the heavy fighting in Afghanistan, miraculously without loss.

October 22nd.

I KNOW nothing quite so dispiriting as indecision. Am not normally given to it, my subconscious seems to get to work on problems, and, without any great soul-searching, I follow intuition. But the past weekend has been and is still one long hell of dither. Shall I, or shall I not buy Robert's grey horse Percy?

Diana, who is on the positive side of the debate, but has a sharp instinct for the practical, put the killer question. "Do you really want to saddle yourself with another horse, and have all the labour of hunting from home, when you get so many rides on other people's horses anyway?". The short answer is "No!"; but then comes the thought that I don't want to turn my back on adventure and excitement yet, I'm not ready to wind down and settle for a quiet life.

He is obviously a young man's ride, but what's the point of life if you don't act daft occasionally? I liked the horse, am in love with him in fact, but Saturday's hunting failed to answer one question, there was no jumping, and raised another, would Percy ever settle down and give me a quiet ride?

IT HAD been pitch dark when I walked round to Church Farm before dawn that morning, frosty, beautiful starlight. Crossing our stable yard I was reminded of how my father took me out there one night more than half a century ago to show me how to identify the Pole Star.

On the path that runs under our garden wall to the churchyard, 'the way of the dead', I could for once have done without an owl's accompaniment – I was unusually nervous, wondering if I had bitten off more than I could chew, and what adventures the morning ahead might bring. I didn't need Wise Owl's mournful *obbligato*.

A grey horse is at least easy to find at night, even if he is likely to need a lot of cleaning once you catch him. But Percy did not put me to the trouble of searching his field for him, he came to the gate when I switched his stable light on, and, after only a slight demur, and a few uncertain side-steps at the approach of a stranger, let me halter him. He stood as quiet, docile and friendly as you could wish whilst I groomed and saddled him: so far so good.

I don't carry a watch, haven't done so for years, and it was a puzzle to know exactly when to start our twenty minutes' hack to Osehill Green – that same farm where I was so reluctantly dragged for dancing a few nights back – I didn't want to be on the road in full darkness, nor yet to be late at the meet. A cock's crow from Julia's hen shed decided it, no doubt it was the same Lavender beauty that so startled me when saddling up before. Off into the gloom Percy and I strode.

∽◅⌇

HE DIDN'T like the half light one little bit, and I wondered if we were even going to get the length of Locks Lane. He spooked at any patch of discolouring on the tarmac, ran sharply back, had to be firmly urged forward; then lost his composure completely when we got to the houses as their security lights leapt officiously into life.

It was a sticky start. I was almost on the point of getting off and leading him, but we at last made what officials call our High Street, and I started to worry about traffic and headlights. Luckily the road was empty, so much so that I began to wonder if I had the right morning and the right meet. But, as we crossed the Caundle Brook at Fox's Bridge, leaving the South Dorset's famed Tuesday country and entering on Blackmore & Sparkford Vale territory, the first of several horse boxes rolled by, and the sun came up. We had arrived: as had the start of my 100th outing in the role of hunting correspondent.

From the moment that Percy realised that hunting was on the menu, until I got him home some four hours later, he gave me not a moment's rest. The snaffle bit in his mouth was no lie, he was easy enough to stop, and there was no real harm in his nervous playfulness, no estrapade, no suggestion of a buck or rear. (An estrapade, by the way, in case you are reaching for the dictionary, is a conscious attempt by a horse to get rid of its rider.)

Percy had worn me to a thread, but, for all his fidget and activity, he was a comfortable ride (not a twinge next day); I felt that he was a kind horse and that he knew his business. I was still at least half in love with him. This had been his first outing with hounds after a long lay-off. If he would but show me that he could settle, and provided we saw eye to eye on how to tackle timber fences, he might very well do. Robert and I agreed that I should give him a second, final trial.

I have never been more shattered by a morning in the saddle, nor come home less ready to sit down to write 1,500 words. I had kindly been given a lift home from the ensuing Hunt Breakfast in a friend's horse-box. When they dropped me in the centre of the village, stepping the long way down from the cab, and backwards, I tripped on the War Memorial curb, fell flat on the grass verge, crushing the glasses case, and, what was even more important, the tape-recorder in my jacket pocket.

My pocket memory had nothing whatever to say to me when, sitting down to sort out my ideas, I consulted it. Fortunately it's just a back-up, I have never entirely relied on it: disgusted, I flung it in the bin.

That was my first, and let's hope will be my last, fall of the season.

October 23rd.

"When I came opposite Lydden Spring the mare turned her head
that way as if she wanted to drink. I let her go in, and she drank;
I thought she would never finish. While she was drinking the
Clock of Newton Buckton church struck twelve."

SO, chequebook in pocket, I set off this morning, in much the same style, for a make-or-break morning with the South Dorset. We had longer to go, a good hour's hack, but, mercifully, the meet was not until 8am. No frost this time, and no spooky Locks Lane to cope with, we set out across Stonylongs, then took Park Lane south over the dawn-lit shoulder of Dungeon, heading for Buckland Newton and beyond.

A pair of fully grown roe scampered away over the hedge as we rose the hill, then a roar behind us warned of the enormous milk-tanker on its morning run. However carefully driven, that long monster can scare the wits out of you in a narrow lane, it makes such a din, and takes such an age to pass. Percy was steadiness itself. It was another useful test. He was walking out beautifully: I was beginning to feel quite bullish about the enterprise.

It is a route so full of memories. In Spring Grove we passed the cottage where the Duntish Estate gamekeeper, Mr Haines, once lived. My father used to send my older brother and me out with him, to get us used to handling guns, and see if we might have a taste for shooting. I did go through a brief shooting phase, but I was useless at it; it never stuck.

The clock on the tower of Buckland Newton church gave us twenty minutes, we were, by chance, spot-on time, if not early. Making a choice of two routes, I turned down, past the loveliest house in the county, what was once the rectory – my father nearly bought it – past the stables, now a dwelling, where we kept our horses when we first moved to Dorset, crossed the infant River Lydden, to the one-time doctor's house, my late childhood and early boyhood, home.

No sign now of the two-roomed wooden shack that was the surgery-cum-waiting room, where my father saw those of his patients that he did not visit in their homes, did all his own dispensing, where I used to sit with him endlessly, talking of this and that, 'helping' him with a move in the postal chess game that he usually had on the go with an old author friend. No doubt, if it were winter, we would discuss the last or the next day's hunting. No-one would dream of practising medicine in such a hovel, or in such a style, today…. more's the pity.

A few paces on, through the garden hedge, I was glad to see, still there, though it has lost its thatch roof, the summer house that my father built for me when, at the age of twelve, I was immobilised by rheumatic fever. In fair weather he would carry me daily to it, find time in his busy life to read to me there. Do you wonder that I tend to go on and on about him, and so pity those fecklessly spawned boys who have to grow up without a father?

⤳⤳

OUT of Buckland, up Hilling Lane, we were soon at Henley, and nearly arrived. In the old council houses at Henley there used to live a cobbler, who mended all the family's shoes and played the trombone, I'll remember his name in a minute, it began with a 'C'.

He had very strong, and wrong-headed, views about Elgar, was violently against his music for some reason, and, to my mother's dismay, would hold forth about it at the Worker's Education Association musical appreciation classes that were held in our house – difficult to imagine in the TV age. We had regular poetry and play-reading sessions for our neighbours too, in those immediately post-war years.

I fancy that cobblers, like millers and blacksmiths, monopolists with a skill that people needed, developed independent characters in old village life. One thinks of Hans Sachs in Wagner's *Meistersingers*, but Mr Caldecott (there, memory has done its work), though making a pretence of being curmudgeonly, was a dear really. He lent me his brass trombone, and I taught myself to play it, well enough to manage 'God Save the King'.

Why and how did the word 'cobblers' acquired its pejorative sense, as meaning 'nonsense', as my mother might have wished to use it? Brewers Dictionary, usually such a reliable fall-back, leaves us guessing. It merely confines itself to telling us that 'Cobbler's punch is gin and water, with a little treacle and vinegar' and 'Cobbler's toast, schoolboy's bread and butter, toasted on the dry side and eaten hot'.

⤳⤳

PADDY, with his quad-bike and terriers was the only, but welcome, evidence in Lanscombe Lane that a meet of foxhounds was due. But soon fol-

– 122 –

lowers gathered on horseback and on foot, the hunt's massive lorry drove up, Rory and our new Whipper-in Richard, decanted their horses, hounds made their joyful entry and we were off.

"Is that Robert's horse?" Rory asked – he didn't actually need telling – "Is that the horse that won the race?" asked another. I had a strong and relevant memory of that occasion. A broken stirrup-leather had held up the start. Percy, not appreciating the delay, had looked difficult to sit, dangerous almost, during what seemed like an age. His lady jockey a courageous neighbour, a pea on a drum, or a robin on a round of beef as my mother used to say, had done wonders sitting him, before going on to steal the race.

Would Percy settle, temperamentally *could* he settle, were the questions? If he wouldn't go quietly with hounds after an hour's hack he was not the horse for me. The long and the short of it was that he didn't, couldn't, wouldn't... at least not to my bidding. I had felt on Saturday that I was an old man on a young man's horse; this wasn't a jot better.

It was worse if anything. Although he has a good mouth, I could stop him, and, as I had noticed with pleasure on the road, he answered well to the voice, in company he tore away full speed given any chance, and would not stand quiet for a second. At one stage he frightened me, a buck seemed just around the corner, not an amusing thought with a horse of that size at my age.

Very sadly, but with my mind made up, after not much more than an hour, I brought him, away from hounds, crabwise down the steep side of Buckland Knoll, objecting all the way, into Castle Lane, and took him home. An absolutely lovely horse, he is too good and too strong for me. I shall always think of him with regret: he very soon found another buyer.

XII

October 25th.

"SAINT Aldhelm no doubt managed without a microphone when he held forth in his Abbey a millennium ago, so why on earth should I have to use one?", was the bolshie question in my head as I wound down Dancing Hill into Sherborne this morning. I have to speak in the abbey, Dorset's 'Cathedral', at a memorial service there tomorrow: this morning I planned to make a recce of 'the field of battle'.

For once I don't dread the occasion. I know exactly what I intend to say, and I am grateful for the chance to say it. My sister's sister-in-law, a dear and valued friend, has been stolen away by the usual thief, well before her time. I had known her since she was nobbut ten or eleven years old.

Sherborne tip was, as usual, my first port of call. I was, again as usual, too early, and joined a queue of cars waiting for it to open. The car wireless had 'Yesterday in Parliament' on, some minister was twittering on in the new dead language, full of 'issues' and 'isms', that politicians love but no normal person uses: nine o'clock struck and I found myself in Colonel Mustard mode. Thirty-plus years in the Army ill-equips you for putting up with sloppiness: I strode forth to find out why the place had not been opened on time, and met one of the staff making his leisurely and apparently unapologetic way to admit us.

I always enjoy the camaraderie at Sherborne tip. We who use it belong to the old, provident, mannered, school, salute each other as we give way in the single-file approach road, try to do what is right by our rubbish, exchange pleasantries, as we rather shame-facedly con over the bargains on display for sale (it's where, for 50p, I got the 'Canaletto' that hangs in my dressing room, and, for a similar sum, my invaluable porter's trolley).

As well as priceless bargains, that is where you can count on finding dear old England these days.... at the rubbish dump, where courtesy rules, and one escapes the warthog world of frown, grab, grudge and grunt.

∽◦∾

THEY were adamant at the Abbey, that I must use the wretched PA system, even though, as I told them, I had in the past addressed hundreds of soldiers from the mudguard of a tank in the open air – never a word missed, as far as I know (Colonel Mustard had evidently not quite returned to his box).

The occasion came back to me rather vividly. We were on a training area in north Germany, had lost a soldier, drowned, driving his tank, when it dived into a bog on a night march I had set his squadron. He was a gutsy boy, all the Regiment knew him from a recent performance in the boxing ring. I felt that we would all be down-in-the-mouth about it, that something needed to be done and said.

I think, I hope, I said it… tomorrow would be something on the same lines. Try to say the right thing, above all be heard. I shall brief someone at the back of the congregation to raise a hand if I'm inaudible.

✇

THURSDAY is my usual Sherborne day, it's when my articles come out, when I get to read them first, see how they have been illustrated. Also, if I'm lucky, I get to read *The Times* in Olivers, the Cheap Street coffee shop – they only have one copy, if it is engaged I perch vulture-like nearby, ready to swoop.

Today I have other reading matter, *Horse & Hound's* annual 'hunting special' issue is out, and I've no fewer than nine pages in it. Why should anybody care but me, but it is a big thrill, the most that I have ever had out in one magazine in one day?

The section opens with what we call a 'feature article', possibly the most difficult I ever had to write, and closes with five pages of the best possible pictures with my account of Saturday morning's hunting – it was little short of a miracle, their getting it out inside four days, to my eyes perfectly, although no doubt others, with sharper eyes, will find mistakes.

The feature article was called 'Fantasy Hunting'. It had required me to ask a dozen huntsmen whose boots they would like to borrow for a day, what their dream hunt was, past or present. I hate the telephone, and have too great a respect for huntsmen to enjoy bothering them with what seemed a footling, not to say insulting, question. Writing it was hell: I almost gave up.

Yet I felt really pleased with the result. It was an example of teamwork, and the Commissioning Editor's art – she knew what she wanted, and how it would look finally on the page. My part was to beaver away, as it were blind, underground, and extract the ore she needed.

On a whim, and feeling high almost, I drove home via Folke, the village so familiar from my boyhood where Jo, whom I was to attempt to eulogise next day, grew up. There was Little Folke, my sister's first married home, the Manor House, Jo's old home, looking just as it did when I used to go regularly there to play squash with her redoubtable father in the barn, and the church where she worshiped (locked… black mark! What is the point of a church you cannot enter at need, on the moment?).

I took the old road home. Broke Lane was little more than a cart track when I first knew it, with Wizard's Bridge, so hump-backed that you could barely cross it in a car. So full of memories that lane is, of the pony that, changing owners, first brought our two families together, brought my sister the best of husbands, him the best of wives, and me two true friends, brother and sister, now both gone.

October 26th.

YOU can never hope to get away with anything in a country neighbour-hood, it's vain to try. I haven't confessed it yet in these pages, let alone to Diana, but Percy and I had had a narrow squeak on the road on the way to hunting last Saturday. It was misty, and still barely light, when, just before leaving the road to gain the meet, I had turned back to give directions to a horse-box driver who was plainly lost, and had overshot.

There was not much room. As I bent to speak to the driver though his cab window a car sped towards us, Percy sidestepped onto the verge, it just squeezed by, lights, and I imagined, driver, ablaze. It was foolish, a close shave, and entirely my own fault.

This morning, my friend the newspaperman arrived as we were at the mounting block, taking an early ride before the day's excitements. It was misty again, he told me of a narrow escape he had had with the hunt in similar conditions on Saturday morning, when he nearly struck a horse.

I confessed that it was Percy, with me on board: we had a laugh about it. He said that I ought to wear one of those fluorescent yellow waistcoats. "Whose side are you on?" I called from the saddle, "Diana's always trying to make me wear one of those beastly things!". "They cost next to nothing in Mole Valley" was his parting shot.

AS you may guess, we were in good time taking our seats in the Abbey that afternoon, and had let ourselves in for an agonizingly long wait, relieved only by gorgeous music as the great nave steadily filled behind us.

"It's just like waiting to ride in a point-to-point"; "You'll be alright once you start"; "That's not *my* experience of point-to-points!", was our whispered exchange, as the moment at last drew close, the clergy processing. At least I was the first to speak, and was on early, after we had sung 'Christ, whose glory...", a comfort surely to the bereaved, supposing they are within reach of comfort.

My brief was to speak about my old friend's love of country life, and to speak for no more than a couple of minutes, I began and ended thus....

"One memorable Christmas holidays sixty years ago I found myself following a pretty girl on a pony across the Blackmore Vale, she had long auburn hair down her back, to her waist almost ... she went like a bird.

Jo was riding Wisdom, and I was on Wizzy's old stable-mate, her brother Guy's outgrown pony, which is no doubt why I was able to keep on terms with her. That pony was responsible for bringing our two families together, and led to a very happy marriage: as some of you will know. That was my earliest memory of Jo – trying to keep up with her across the Vale. As you can see, it has never left me.....

....When, on the last day of 2002, my brother-in-law Guy unexpectedly died, I was at my wits end to know how best to help my sister to shoulder that sudden, dreadful burden, her children and grand-children all in Oz. It's at times like that you get the true measure of a friend. Jo knew exactly what to do and how to do it: she gave me a lead once more. We crossed that tricky bit of country together. Again, as she always did… Jo went like a bird."

"Now boast thee, death, in thy possession lies
A lass unparallel'd".

October 27th.

"CAN'T horses count?" I ask myself, "surely ours know by now that I only have two bits of apple for each of them?", but they go at me like piranha, most unhelpfully, whilst I struggle Bella and Harvey into their head-collars to bring them in for work.

We are nipping out for an early ride before guests depart and arrive: it's a busy time. Emma, one of the several Australian great-nieces that Jo and I shared, was staying with us overnight, following the memorial service. She slept in her grandmother's, my sister's, old room, which had been once *her* grandmother's room – five generations in this house, I begin to feel that we quite belong here!

∽∾∾

MUCH of the 'Farming Programme' on the wireless this morning was devoted to badgers, and the plague that those lovely animals have so sadly been allowed to become, and the fact that no minister or government has the guts to do anything about it. I had been very struck by a letter on the subject in *The Times* that I read on Thursday in Olivers, so struck in fact that I for once bought a copy of the paper, brought it home, and cut the letter out.

One of self-defeating things about the endless stream of 'news' and comment in the media is that we can never dwell on anything. We are invited to take an interest, raise our hands in horror, and then immediately move on and forget all about it. Here, to share my tiny slice of posterity, is what that writer from Rutland had to say…

"There is an important issue that has been totally lost in the debate over the culling of the badger and whether this animal causes TB in cattle. I would ask the question: Should badgers be a protected species at all now?

When I became a farmer35 years ago, badgers were not present on my 125-hectare farm. In the time since they became a protected species, the population has grown to the point where they can be legitimately be regarded as the main pest.

Many areas of the country have more serious problems of overpopulation than Leicestershire.

I have on my farm a badger population of several hundred animals living in ten separate setts. This animal population is equivalent in 'species pressure' to a flock of 75 sheep. Badgers have no natural predators, and, other than the danger from motorcars, are vigorously protected. Numbers continue to increase beyond the point where the species is in balance with the environment around it. Because of the vigorous feeding nature of the badger, there is scarcely a square metre of the farm (or village gardens) that does not bear evidence of their numbers.

Ground nesting birds and farm cattle are the most obvious losers from this huge man-made imbalance in nature, although effects on growing crops and other habitat can be observed. Before the protection of the badger species, it was certainly over-controlled by Man: it is now under-controlled. The reduction of the badger population in this country is not just about TB control, but about sensible wildlife management".

We don't, I believe, have quite such an infestation of badgers in Dorset as they evidently do in Leicestershire, but it is bad enough. In my lifetime I have seen that fine animal transformed by urban sentimentality and ignorant, not to say meddling and mischievous politicians, into a pest.

DISASTER struck as we returned from our short ride. Coming down Stock Hill, passing the Manor and nearly home, a dead ash tree was on the point of being felled in the field beside the road. The crew hadn't noticed us: a tractor was straining at a steel hawser secured high in the tree's crown: a chainsaw was already busy.

I turned to Diana to urge her to hurry Harvey forward. Trotting down the gently sloped road he went suddenly dead lame, on that same leg with the tweaked tendon. We got home safely, before the tree crashed, but our little world had fallen in. All our hopes for Harvey, all the care Diana had lavished on him since he injured himself in May, all my teeth-grinding patience, had gone for nothing. He looks like a dead loss.

October 27th.

SUNDAY is the best day for selling poppies: nearly everybody is at home. In some ways it's a sad business, after a twelvemonth gap many of my regulars are so obviously a year older, take that much longer to get to the door, and then to find their money, and return with it. Also, you can't do proper justice to the occasion – many of them don't get a lot of callers, would like a good chat, have known me since a boy: but you just can't dwell on every doorstep, let alone accept an invitation to step in. You feel bad about it, but must move on.

There are the usual puzzles. How do you make your presence known when a front door sports neither bell nor knocker, and there is no dog to announce you? Rattling the letter-flap seldom does the trick, nor does rapping the, usually glass, upper panel. I don't know the answer, won't know next year, nor the year after. It's a perennial problem.

Neglected soldiers are in the news. People are extraordinarily generous, banknotes from people who can be by no means flush for cash: I sense another record take – as I had last year.

⥲∞⥲

MATINS had brought a facer: I don't know when I was so fed up. Margaret our organist, a keen beagler, who had been in the Abbey on Friday, told me that she'd hardly heard a word of what I said. Michael, our stand-in rector, who had been sitting near her, said the same. What an exercise in futility, I felt like 'Bill the Lizard' (see below).

You, sweat blood, really put your heart into stringing the right words together, rehearse them, and they go unheard because of some gremlin in that wretched PA system that they would have me use! I was not just fed up, but furious.

As well as being maddening it was a mystery. My 'spy' in the furthest back pew, what looked like a quarter of a mile distant from the pulpit, greeted me with the kindest of smiles and assurances as we left: she had promised me to raise a hand if she was not hearing properly.

Many people at the tea party in the Big Schoolroom, after the service, said that they had heard every word, and Diana would have been the first to complain if what I had said had not come across clearly.

There was evidently a local blind, deaf, or dumb spot in a section of one side of the nave; one of the loudspeakers was not functioning. You may be sure that Colonel Mustard did not waste any time in making his feelings know to 'Rev. Green'.

> "One of the jurors had a pencil that squeaked. This, of course,
> Alice could not stand, and she went round behind him, and
> very soon found an opportunity of taking it away.
> She did it so quickly that the poor little juror
> (it was Bill, the Lizard) could not make out at all what
> had become of it; so, after hunting all about for it,
> he was obliged to write with one finger for the rest of the day;
> and this was of very little use, as it left no mark on the slate".

October 30th.

WITH the vet due later in the week it seemed sensible to try Dandy under the saddle this morning, to see if he was still lame in the shoulder, after several weeks of rest. He walked off well enough, trotted sound on Stonylongs, and was, as he always is, a trifle uneven at the trot on the road. Certainly his shoulder was not troubling him: so far so good.

By a stroke of luck Colin and his tractor driver Karen came riding down Park Lane towards us; they judged Dandy sound too. Close behind them came a horsebox, and the penny dropped… it's Tuesday, hounds are in the village, Colin and Karen were heading for the meet; they must have thought it odd, my riding off in the opposite direction.

Wanting to check my pitch for litter, I made on up to the Dungeon Hill gateway, before turning for home. Halfway back, and off Dandy to pick up a plastic bottle that some charmer had chucked down in the road, the meet traffic started to hot up. Hastily stuffing the offensive item in my jacket pocket I climbed the bank to regain the saddle.

It's amazing how horses contrive to make a fool of you, especially when there is an audience; they have a genius for it. As I went to reach for the stirrup the plastic horror in my pocket went "Crackle-pop!". Dandy shied off to the length of the reins, completely blocking the road, holding up the traffic, and dragging me off the bank. We must have looked a comic pair whilst I restored order, but I suppose that it gave members of the field something to laugh about at the meet.

The hound lorry was the next to pass us; as usual it was loud with cries of lamentation, expectancy and querulous complaint. Dandy lit up, suddenly the picture of bustling health, and carried me smartly home.

November 1st.

"Behold, there ariseth a little cloud out of the sea,
like a man's hand"

THE VET came this morning, gave Harvey a thorough going over, endless trotting-up and lunging, with nothing to show for it, not a touch of lameness. The upshot is that we are to continue working him and see what happens. There was the most gorgeous sunset as I went out to take the horses off the strip grazing, give them their rations for the night, and say good bye to them.

It has been a crowded time. Yesterday was our annual Bath day (please note the capital letter); we saw a wonderful production of *Nicholas Nickleby*; tomorrow, at dawn, we set off for Scotland and the Borders where I am to write up two hunts, on Saturday and Monday, and speak at a hunt dinner in a castle. I had intended to do four hunts, but, thank goodness, sense dawned. Even now I fear that I may have over-faced myself, and as usual, the dinner scares me stiff.

It all started, 'the little cloud arose', at the Gentlemen at Arms cocktail party, in the garden of Clarence House, in May. An old army friend and polo enemy asked if I would write-up a day with the Berwickshire this season. I light-heartedly agreed, put together a mini-tour, got a couple of Editors squared, then he dumped this dinner thing on me.

As usual, Diana exclaimed "Why didn't you say 'No!'?": as usual, I replied "I didn't feel that I could". I think that you have heard all this before. All that I can say is that I am looking forward to looking back on it...

November 2nd – 6th.

"Rot ye, Sir!" he exclaims, "hangin's too good for ye! You should be condemned to hunt in Berwickshire the rest of your life".

.... I'm not sure what I was worrying about, we had a wonderful tour and I had two brilliant horses to ride. I was scared almost out of my wits at one stage, but in my trade you expect that: indeed you hope for it, you've got to have something to write about.

The scary bit was with the Berwickshire; writing the day up for *Country Life* I called it 'The Incident at Toot Corner'. Driving me to the meet, my friend and host Charles Ramsay had pointed out the said corner, a hairpin bend in a narrow road that snaked down through close woodland to Abbey St Bathan's, by the River Whiteadder. We were in the foothills of the Lammermuirs, the Berwickshire's high country. How could I know that Toot Corner was to become a spot that I shall never forget: it is just as well not to have foreknowledge in my line of work?

The horse they gave me to ride was a magnificent 13-year-old, seventeen-hand eventer called Peregrine. I could not have asked for better, and since the field master was riding Peri's stable-mate, I just had to fasten on to his coat-tails to enjoy a busy carefree jumping morning. We were on turf, the sun was shining, the views just stunning; the whole thing was heaven.

Even heaven palls of course. As the early afternoon wore on, after several active hours in the saddle, I found myself again and again glancing up at the sun, secretly hoping to see it close with the skyline, praying that it would drop. Every time I covertly looked that way it just didn't seem to have moved.

The Autumn colours were stupendous: they had been, all the way up the length of the country as we had driven north on the day before: Winter seems to have gone AWOL, no doubt it will turn up sometime. However the most memorable view of the day was looking down onto a circular Victorian Gothic house called The Retreat, built I was told by the Earl of Wemyss, who had kept the hounds there when he was MFH in the mid-nineteenth century.

The circular ground plan of The Retreat, no doubt consciously, echoed that of a remarkable structure on the hill above, Edin's Hall Broch, the southernmost of Scotland's Pictic brochs. As the sun at last dropped below Cockburn Law, I was tempted to enter this awesome, prehistoric structure. Peri stepped delicately through the rock-strewn entrance, and there, on that wondrous spot, our day ended.

A friendly-looking gently descending grass path was pointed out as being the way home. We were to find a ford and a wicket in the wood at the bottom, and then the road beyond. Nobody said those fatal words, but they hung in the air, "You can't miss it!": we did, we went badly wrong.

Led by my host, half-a-dozen of us descended what proved, suddenly, but after it was too late to turn back, to be a terrifyingly dwindling path, treacherous with half-fallen trees overhead and no more than fleeting, slithering ground for our horses' hooves to find purchase on.

The burn, when we achieved it, was profoundly uninviting, the wicket narrow, to be taken in a sloshing up-hill kangaroo leap, and then, unbelievably, a flight of steps was to be climbed, about thirty of them, to emerge at Toot Corner. We were evidently on a footpath: I question that a horse had ever been that way before. Even though Peri took it all very sensibly, I cannot remember being more thoroughly scared; on a big horse, there just was not room for a missed foothold, or error of any sort.

I felt quite good about it afterwards, the way one does after surviving a shaking: it had been a very, very happy if rather long day in the saddle. But it was 11.30 that evening before I was on my feet at Wedderburn Castle, near Duns, to speak at the Hunt Dinner. That was torture, I didn't feel good about *that* at all; they'll have to get up very early in the morning to trick me into that sort of caper again.

THE Sunday morning had to be given over to writing up the previous day, and getting it out of my head, before we set off for Hexham, prior to spending Monday, Guy Fawkes Day, out with the Border Hunt.

Understandably, Editors are loath to let you return again and again to the same hunt. My pretext for a fourth visit, to this my favourite hunting country and favourite pack, was that the father, in a remarkable father-and-son Mastership, Ian Hedley, was 95 years old. The plan was that I would interview him whilst we were being driven to the meet.

This worked better than most plans do; my new pocket recorder actually worked; I got some wonderful 'copy'. It was thrilling listening to the old man tell of how the 10th Duke of Northumberland asked him, a tenant farmer, to take the pack on in 1952, of the various triumphs and disasters during his 21 seasons hunting his hounds, before his son Michael took over, and of the ways and characters of the Border shepherds, whose livelihoods the hunt exists to protect, and whose active support of hunting is indispensable.

I was expecting to ride a locally well-known white cob called Mr McGoo, which sounded a safe enough ticket for that trappy country, and was rather disconcerted when a tall five-year-old was led out for me; Mr McGoo being evidently off-games for some reason. I needn't have worried, Morgan, with Irish Draft blood in his veins, proved to be wise for his years: his grandsire was King of Diamonds, which meant that he was some sort of half- or step-nephew of my own beloved and much missed Woody, the best horse I ever owned.

IT was to be another long day in the saddle, without any jumping this time, but the wind was tremendous, quite disconcerting when it suddenly hit you at a crest. Looking around me as we quit the meet, my eye was caught by a distinctive figure of an oldish man on a blue-roan pony. "That's the pilot for me" I thought, and tagged along as he climbed Hindhope Law. It was soon apparent that, as can so easily happen in that country, we had bet on the wrong hill. Hounds, and most of the field were away off, out of view, in a vast stretch of forestry.

Climbing down off Hindhope Law, grateful to my pilot for much engaging conversation and for opening several gates, if not for leading me onto the wrong hill, a lady met on foot with a familiar blue cashmere scarf and a whippet turned out to be Diana. The dog, touchingly like our own long lost Perdita, was borrowed from our hosts of the previous evening, who had somehow managed to get their party much nearer to hounds than *Horse & Hound's* all-knowing correspondent had. Ian Hedley was there too, also on foot of course: he had hollered, and been delighted that his old hounds had come to him.

Meeting an old friend, an artist and musician well remembered from an earlier Border raid, I switched pilots… but soon regretted it. She led off down the next 'mountain', into the gale, going a lot faster that I found comfortable.

Steeper and steeper we went, the wind buffeting us mercilessly, until a near perpendicular place where I really could not see what looked like one single sensible foothold. Praying that he and Mary Ann, my pilot, knew what they were doing, I just let Morgan get on with it. As you can see, we survived.

IT WAS well past two o'clock, with the sun beginning to think about bed, that Morgan and I found ourselves alongside the Huntsman, back above the meet, on Hindhope Hill. He had just blown his horn, almost for the first time since we moved off. He and his hounds, in Blackie Hope below us, were both thoroughly aware of each other, but Michael was as ever "letting them work it out for themselves".

A wisp of hounds, four or five of them, amongst them Gallant, Wagtail and Trophy, as if uncertain where their duty lay, were by us, alternately gazing adoringly up at Michael, and then down at the doings of the remainder of the pack.

It was a moment to savour being out with those hounds and in that unique country. The sun doesn't always shine of course, huntsmen wouldn't wish it, but now you could see out over mile upon mile of spectacular, open, muscular hills. To our south Northumberland, with the 'English fence' on the skyline, to the north I fancied I could see out of Roxburghshire into Berwickshire, to the Lammermuirs of Saturday's adventures.

The strong smell of cheese in the air was from the wild goats behind us – wild indeed they looked, lots of them, some with enormous horns. Cheviot ewes seemed to be line-dancing on the far slope, on Gaisty Law. I never saw such an endless string of sheep, anxiously processing, first this way, then that.

The mounted field were in clumps on their chosen vantage points, here and there, each group taking a punt on which was the best place to be, ready for the next move. There is no field master of course, you go where you please with the Border Hunt... and where else can you stand alongside the Huntsman, following what is going on as he thinks aloud? Do you wonder I have returned so often?

Soon the activity and sounds below us decided Gallant & Co as to where their duty lay, and we also were drawn down off the hill. The field now gathered where the foot followers had taken their stand, close by the meet. Michael blew for his hounds, as, like the mounted field, they came in dribs and drabs. Another day was over.

"Do those old hills have memories?" I had wondered as we stood, in my case almost certainly for the last time, above Hindhope. "Do they remember a small boy on a Shetland pony, with a sack for a saddle, riding there the best part of a century ago?"

"Do they recall how, when a man, Ian Hedley hunted his hounds there for twenty-one seasons, and how he and his son built up one of the best packs of foxhounds going? And will they always remember, as I shall, the echo of Michael's wild "Hai! Hai! Hai!", as he cheers those staunch allies of the Border shepherds to their work?"

XIII

November 8th – 11th.

"MUST you wear that tie, it clashes with your trousers?" Diana had asked as we got ready to go out for a rather daunting luncheon party. I have no sense of colour, and am quite often sent upstairs to change before we go out. But the answer on this occasion was "Yes: I can't wear any other tie today". It was Remembrance Sunday: it was my regimental tie.

The Eliott trews I wore in honour of my mother, as an act of defiance to show that I wasn't overawed by the company that we were going to keep, and to tease our hosts, who bear that name, though they spell it differently. My distant forebears on my mother's side were Border Reivers, that is to say cattle thieves. The name is spelt four different ways, depending how you juggle or double the consonants, it's important to get it 'right'. Monday's hunting had begun and ended in an Elliot kitchen.

At lunch I found myself sitting next to the widow of one prime minister, my vis-à-vis the former wife of the grandson of another; I leave you to work out who was who. It was a brush with history; also present were sundry in-the-swim people from the literary, political and media world. Diana and I were out of our depth, but I think we kept afloat, more-or-less got away with it. It was great fun; the champagne before lunch was an enormous help.

"There is, perhaps, no greater hardship at present inflicted on mankind in civilised and free countries, than the necessity of listening to sermons."

EARLIER in the week I had had a brief speaking part at the induction service for our new Rector, in Bishop Caundle's parish church. I had to hand him a bible, King James's of course, and express the hope that it would be "a lamp to our feet and a light upon our path"; a good strong phrase in the best sort of monosyllabic English, I wonder where it comes from?

There was an interval of panic during the hymn before I had to step forward; it was a 'tweedledum' moment. The choir was full of robed clergy, some of whom looked rather alike. However, I'd sorted our man out before the music stopped, and all went well.

It was a lovely service, throughout which my gaze was continually drawn to a grandson of the new incumbent, called Abraham, who was lying in a Moses basket in the pew in front. Barely a yard separated our faces. He looked preternaturally sage, as babies do, half smiling when I sang.

A very young-looking bishop was in charge, an impressive man, with an excellent voice, just the sort of voice a bishop ought to have. He showed his youth by preaching with great verve and enthusiasm but, in my very humble opinion, for rather too long! It's a pity clergymen aren't under the same discipline as to time in the pulpit as we journalists are for space on the page.

As usual, we watched the Albert Hall ceremony on the Saturday evening, with the usual feelings, and the Cenotaph service and march-past next day. It is impossible to watch those old servicemen's proud profiles, and the mien of the splendid women who supported them, without feeling hope welling up, as well as pride. We are, surely, the same people: sooner or later we will, we must surely, come the need, find ourselves again.

November 15th.

WINTER has reported in for duty, stamping its boots and presenting arms officiously; last night we had the first really heavy frost, the ground turned to iron. Trees that were previously in denial surrendered immediately, dropping their leaves ankle deep where I cleared up only yesterday.

The vegetable garden is in shock, each broad bean plant, yesterday standing up so proud, is a drooping penitent, the broccoli, only recently in leaf again after being pillaged by cabbage-white caterpillars, is in mourning, and even those hardy soldiers, my leeks, never known to grumble or complain, look chastened. They had all perked up by the time I went to lock the church in the evening, but there were still patches of frost lingering here and there: I have a feeling that we may be in for it.

I work on the principle that you only have to burn a leaf once, so I try to keep on top of what is surely one of the worst outdoor chores of the year, clearing the leaves up as they drop. Diana recently asked "Why don't you just leave them where they fall?". It's a good question, and I mean to find out. I have mentally marked two well covered trees, and mean to note exactly what does happen to their dead leaves between now and next spring.

IF I haven't mentioned our own horses much recently it is because things are so dire in the stables, particularly with Harvey, I try not to think about them when I'm not actually with them. Dandy seems permanently slightly lame, not painfully so, but stiff, arthritic perhaps; I ride him gently, occasionally, for old times' sake, coming home each time with the thought that I probably will have his shoes off next time Duffy calls, and not ride him again.

Bella is still a joy to ride, athough, each morning, I dread to find that her hind leg has swollen up again. Recently we went on the hill and through Hay Wood looking for two orange Sainsbury shopping bags that had somehow slipped their moorings at my saddle-Ds – intended for litter, they had, to my shame and rage, themselves become litter. So far we have recovered only one of them.

The last time Diana and I were able to ride out together, before Harvey finally went sick, as we were climbing onto Dungeon a Chinook helicopter flew very low, unusually low, almost below us, across the village. Living as we do in a low-fly zone, and with Yeovilton a bare few air-minutes off, the horses are inured to the noise, just don't heed it. My thought was "Poor devils! Training to risk their lives in two far off doubtful wars".

"Far-called our navies melt away".

November 17th - 19th.

"Was it a vision or a waking dream?
Fled is the music:- do I wake or sleep?"

THE church bells woke me, just two or three disjointed strokes, no more. For a moment it was a problem to remember where I was, and what might be the time of day. Then it came to me that I was sleeping off last night's dinner party, and getting ready for tonight's. It was mid-afternoon, nearly, but not quite, time for the horses' tea; I dropped off again.

We have Tinker, a neighbour's lurcher, staying with us. Tinker is twelve years old, rough-coated, greyhound size, but otherwise very like his old friend and ours, the late Perdita: he has her beseeching eye and gentle nature, her elegance, and, above all, her pianissimo manner. He is just exactly my sort of dog, and he comes joyfully at the slightest whistle: we seem to appreciate each other's company.

As darkness falls, easing the pressure in a bustling kitchen, he comes with me to lock the church and take a final walk. Once we are in Stonylongs he disappears into the gloom at pace, but just half a whistle, hardly a breath, brings him back flat out, racing round me in circles. He's adorable, a real man's dog.

We are almost home again before I remember those bells – did I really hear them ring? We double back, I unlock the dark church, an uncomfortable childhood memory in my head, either fictional or fact, of someone once hanging himself in a belfry. All the ropes are up, no one has touched them; evidently their 'ringing' was a dream.

IT WAS not difficult to work out where the dream had come from. On the day before we had been at a friend's funeral. Funerals or memorial services tread on each others' heels these days, as is to be expected in the winter of life, but this had been an untimely, sudden, death, a dreadful shock to all concerned.

The widow was a keen bell-ringer, and Crewkerne was alive with the sound of bells as we made our way to a church I had never seen the inside of before. More like a cathedral than a parish church, it was grand, airy, beautiful, with graceful, slender pillars to its nave, and a lot of oak, old ships' timber no doubt, in the vaulting.

Anger effectively distracts from sorrow. During the service my eye was for ever drawn to a 'No Smoking' notice on a nearby table. Is it possible to think of a better example of the State's impudence, waste, ignorance and fiddling idiocy, than to insist on such a notice being displayed in such a place? As if anybody smoked in church!

The wretched thing was in a photograph frame. It was a relief of spirits to slam it on its silly face as we left: I would have liked to have dashed it to the ground.

"Four feet said 'I'm coming with you'
And trotted along behind".

"WOULD you mind taking Tink for his walk instead of riding?", "Why can't I do both?", "The Rays are coming here for bridge tonight"' "Ah!", was the exchange at Monday morning's breakfast table. It had Tinker and me heading across Lady Mead for Great Wootton Wood once I had seen to the horses' breakfast.

When I got to the gate that heads the field there was no sign of him, he'd flown the gate, all of four feet with the drop on the home side, and was away off round the bend in the short droveway beyond. A whistle brought him back. Woody and I used to jump that gate coming home from hunting, it's easy, a mere skip as you come downhill to it: his body language would say "Let's go!", and I'd say "Why not?".

It was breaking two of the unwritten rules of hunting – never lark on the way home, and don't jump your neighbour's gates – but what's the point of life if you don't kick over the traces now and then? I doubt that I would do it these days though, even if I had the horse for it.

Out of the top of the wood, we skirted Dungeon, and cut back illicitly through a meadow and a wood where I wouldn't think of riding, and we had no business walking, gaining Park Lane about halfway down its length.

It was spot where I had thrown a dead badger out of the road, over the hedge, 'back along' (to use a favourite Dorset phrase), perhaps two years ago. There was no sign, not a trace of it – same story with the wretched roe that treed itself late last year, in the hedge further down, not so much as a single bone was left. How tidy Nature is!

Back home nearly, I held the Stonylongs wicket open for Tinker: but, a dog after my own heart, he chose to leap the cattle-grid. Diana was on the telephone when we hit the kitchen, I heard "He has been much better recently"… and, "Mind you, I give him a good talking to every now and then". She and her buddy were evidently discussing yesterday's luncheon party and my social proclivities, or lack of them.

November 26th.

SHOULD you have happened to have seen me at first- or last-light this past week hurrying down the orchard with a small cube of Cheddar cheese gripped between thumb and first-finger, it would have been because checking the mouse-trap in the vestry cupboard has been added to my duties as the month's church key-holder.

To date I have been able to eat the cheese myself, but I live in fear of finding a little corpse, or worse, a little writhing body. Just three more days: my fingers are firmly crossed: I'm rather on the side of mice, although I daren't admit as much to the Church Warden.

Yesterday, Sunday, was chaotic. Diana had accepted a lift to Aintree, to see a neighbour's horse, pleasingly called 'I Hear Thunder', run in the Becher Handicap Chase, a try-out for the Grand National. Eight hours on the road! I told her that I wouldn't have a moment's peace of mind until she was safe home. "How do you suppose I feel, when you go off on your hunting expeditions?", she parried.

I had spent Saturday with the Axe Vale, down by Seaton, wonderfully mounted, such a happy day, marred only by the long drive home, which nearly finished me. They had given me Pikey to ride again. A big skew-bald, Cornish bred by a van horse out of an eventing mare, he was just the horse for that trappy country, and just the horse for me.

If some kind fairy were to offer me the choice of all the wonderful horses I have ridden in recent years, I do believe that Pikey would get my vote. He jumps like a rainbow, so safe and capable, and loves the work. Every now and then he would 'rev up', gather his hocks under him and do a couple of leaps forward, as if asking "Where's the next excitement, where's the fun, let's get there?".

About 3pm, as usual, age was telling: I'd had enough. Pikey's owner, who had got the measure of me, turned with an enquiring eye. I nodded, and she told her daughter to look after me: thus a seven-year-old on her tiny pony took this old man home. She chattered, delightfully, the whole long way, whilst I undid the plaits in Pikey's mane.

For some reason I had been unusually anxious about that day's hunting, in the lead-up, my nerves and my imagination playing silly games. Right up until the moment I was in the saddle I was for some cranky intuitive reason expecting the day to end in disaster. The first jump put a smile on my face, which I don't think ever left it.

Sunday was set aside for writing, for once watching the racing on TV, and worrying about Diana. 'I Hear Thunder' ran heroically, leading part of the way, surviving another horse falling under his feet at Becher's, but lost his jockey somewhere later on the course and didn't finish. Diana came home safely. We were both too tired for Mrs Gaskell's *Cranford*, which is saved for another day. I had wanted to welcome Diana home with an omelette, but there wasn't an egg to be found anywhere in the house...

November 27th.

"No eggs!"

... or anywhere hereabouts, all the local hens seem to have gone off lay; shortage of daylight I suppose. Bella and I visited the egg-banks in Locks Lane and Kennels Lane yesterday, both normally sure finds, and drew them blank.

We had better luck today however. When the hen-mother in Newlands Lane saw me standing dismounted, boggled by the empty egg box at her gate, she ran out to offer all she had, five hen, and two bantam eggs.... for 60p.

I gave her a pound, her children run the poultry business. "I don't give them any pocket money, they have to earn it", Sarah told me. Her husband Guy, an airline pilot, joined us at the gate carrying their youngest, of four. They are a family that is very dear to the village, and to all who know them I would guess.

Riding home, we met, first, Kate, our hunt's field-master, on her way "to recce two of Billy (Sarah's father)'s hedges", then Rory, who hunts the hounds, no doubt on a diplomatic mission to one of the farmers or landowners up the lane. Both stopped to chat, and ask why I wasn't hunting. Again I had forgotten it was Tuesday, our hounds again due in the neighbourhood.

They were round and about right up to nightfall, snatches of their music distracting Dandy and co, and happily colouring our day – except that I wanted to be with them. The church tower seemed the obvious spot to watch from, but I couldn't find the key in its old place under the collection bags in the vestry cupboard – elf-n-safety I suppose – I all but caught my fingers in the mouse-trap vainly searching for it.

November 28th.

"WHEN's the funeral?" neighbours keep asking me as Bella and I meet them about the village. We are all in shock. Gerald went into hospital for an operation: the next thing we heard was that he was dead. I was riding out, hoping for a word with a farmer and long-time resident who had been at school with him, trying to get some ideas into my head as to what to say at my old friend's funeral.

It proved to be a fruitless errand, short of tying Bella up by her reins, a doubtful thing to do, I couldn't get near enough the house to make myself heard, and milking was over; there was no one in the yard. So for the usual reason, which I won't name, I started out on foot for home.

It was hot work. My weather forecast, that we were in for a bout of arctic weather, was way adrift. It has been ridiculously warm, with primroses showing in Park Lane: last week I actually picked a daffodil for the house in the vegetable garden.

Somewhere about half way home, with Bella following me at the full length of her reins, I spotted something in the opposite verge, crossed to retrieve it, when a large blue car came round the corner. There wasn't any danger, and it didn't have to brake or slow, but, as its back view receded, I recognized it as my own. I shall hear more of that later, I'm always in hot water for being a danger in the road.

November 29th.

A SIMPLE cross, made of two short lengths of batten roughly nailed together, marked where the gravediggers were to work. It brought me up short when I went to unlock the church this morning, thinking, "So that's where Gerald is going to lie, next to his old friend George Dunning", not fifty paces from where he lived out his remarkable boyhood. Whatever may eventually replace it, it is difficult to imagine a fitter monument to that good, simple, solid, tough, unpretentious farmer and countryman, or a better paradigm for my 'eulogy'.

"Speak like a soldier" his widow had said, and, in unison with her daughter, "No sympathy please: we won't be able to bear it". I could not have asked for more congenial 'riding instructions'.

Gerald came to the parish first at Michaelmas in 1932, when he was five years old, his father having taken the tenancy of Church Farm, then part of the Castle Hill Estate. Little more than a month later his father was killed, on the level-crossing in Sherborne. He was taking the milk in, as farmers did in those days, when the brakes on the lorry failed, on Gas House Hill.

From that day, with just one, older, sister, Gerald had to grow into being the man of the family. At the hand-inspection at the start of each day in our infant school, I learnt, the teacher used to say, "We won't look at Gerald's hands; he's been milking". So he had, and so he would be again after school, milking by hand of course. My first memory of him, by then a young man in his twenties, is his daily taking the churns down our drive for collection from the stand by the village forge.

When his mother died, Church Farm had to be sold by the Estate, Gerald, married by then, managed another farm in the parish. Early one morning, during milking, he was almost fatally trampled underfoot by a cow.

On his own, with a fractured skull and smashed face, he somehow contrived to switch off the electricity, and drive himself, not to the safety and care of his home, just around the corner, but to Duntish, two miles off, so as to tell the farm owner how things stood in the milking parlour.

Only then did he summon help for himself. He was brought to my father's surgery here, my mother, who had had a nurse's training, was, as always on such occasions, very much to the fore. Three hospitals passed Gerald on, his case too difficult for them, before he was expertly repaired, his skull riveted, in Portland Naval Hospital.

That was almost the only time in seventy years of farming that Gerald troubled the doctors. "He broke an arm once, and once had flu'", Margaret, his widow, told me, "for a week". Then, just after his eightieth birthday, he took us all by surprise by dying. The last thing he did before he went to hospital was to plant out seventy-five young wallflowers – he loved his garden. "They've all taken" Margaret said.

> "His life was gentle, and the elements
> So mix'd in him that Nature might stand up
> And say to all the world, 'This was a man!'"

December 2nd.

THEY have put one of those idiotic 'No Smoking' signs up in our church porch; apparently the Church Wardens were under threat of a heavy fine if they failed to do so. To ease my spirits I turned the wretched thing upside down first thing this morning, wondering if the Bishop will notice; he is due with us, to take the monthly 'children's service'.

Computers have their uses, once Gerald's funeral is over I mean to amend the notice in matching print to read, 'No Smoking, Bicycling or Lap Dancing', with an apologetic footnote reading 'the Churchwardens intend at an early date to post copies of this notice in Urdu, Sanskrit, Arabic, Gaelic, the Welsh Language and Braille', wait to see if anybody spots it, and what happens if they do.

This fiasco of 'no smoking' notices in our churches prompts several questions. What on earth are our spineless hierarchs doing, tamely acquiescing in such an insult to their flock? Are such notices posted in mosques? Is incense still allowed? But whatever we may think of it, this courageous stamping out of the widespread evil of smoking in churches, along with the total abolition of hunting, must, when the history of the past decade comes to be written, rate as one of the great triumphs of the New Labour administration.

⤬

A tremendous gale blew in overnight, from the southwest of course, where all our heavy weather comes from. I fed the horses, for once, in their shelter. It was such a joy seeing the three of them feeding pacifically alongside each other, like cab-horses in stalls.

We are strip-grazing the rich grass that has grown where Neil took our crop of hay this summer. Shifting the fence that morning was like taking in a reef in a heavy sea. The two hundred yards of doubled half-inch electric tape, bellied out in the fierce cross-wind: it was as much as I could do, almost more than I could do, first to anchor it, then to get it into some sort of straight line.

I had all but lost that battle with the ferocious wind, and came back to the house buffeted and giddy, not at all myself, had to sit down for a bit to collect my wits. If I had to put a finger on the calendar to indicate the day on which I first felt old, it would be Advent Sunday 2007.

⤬

IT WAS a 'continental' breakfast that I had given the horses, just one biscuit of their beloved *Horsehage* shared between them, rather that the 'full English' of one biscuit each, because we are gradually acclimatizing them to the rich paddock grass, little-by-little each day. It's all part of the run-up to H day, when Harvey goes for his operation, and starts his (and my) sentence of endless weeks of dreaded box-rest.

After breakfast, the weather was still as wild as wild could be. Greatly daring, instead of leading them over from Chantry Mead, for the first time I let them take themselves out of one gate, twenty paces down Locks Lane, and, through another, into the paddock. Dandy and Bella know the drill of old, but Harvey was, potentially, the joker. It worked perfectly, but I was glad to have the Admiral, by chance just then walking Zulu, his adorable lurcher, blocking the lane in case Harvey should elect to wander.

My niece Rosalind, the King's Troop vet, her husband Duncan, and their nine-month-old Labrador bitch Echo, were staying with us. I trotted Dandy up for Ros's expert (free!) inspection. "Right fore" she said. Clever girl, not everybody immediately sees what I feel riding him!

Later, as we were taking the horses back to their field after their strictly rationed paddock-gobbling spell, she did a flexion test on that leg, holding it up, tight, for 45 seconds, before I trotted him again. Same story, except that it was a bit hectic as we were also holding up the church traffic in Locks Lane, and he was a fraction lamer. "Good news" she said, "It's in the soft tissue" – ie not in the hoof.

– 143 –

Earlier, when we had done the first test, just as I was returning Dandy to the paddock, a car had sped up the drive, clearly lost, looking for the church. I flagged it down... a clerical collar, crimson vest... it was the Bishop again. It's not often you get the chance to give a Right Reverend the right-about!

We were all due to have lunch in Castle Cary. There was the usual kerfuffle getting away. "Where's Echo?" asked her mistress: "She's sitting by the door, waiting to go" came the answer. Don't I just know that feeling: I'm getting rather attached to Echo?

∽∾

IT WAS still blowing half a gale, pitch dark and soaking wet when we got back and I had to struggle out with the night hay. No sign of the horses, but they came sploshing in at the gallop once I had started to load the rack. Chantry Mead is the best-drained field in the parish, but I have never known it wetter, just walking on it you can barely keep your feet.

My day wasn't over. There were lights showing in the church when it should have been long since locked for the night: I couldn't just ignore them, with churches being shamelessly robbed all over the country. Lucy, our senior Church Warden, was helping a hapless mum search for a Paddington Bear, whose owner had lost it that morning: one could all too easily picture the frantic bedtime scene at home, some child's comfort-toy gone AWOL.

It was a comfort to me to notice, as I left, that the 'eleventh commandment' was still standing on its head.

> *"Is it not written, 'My house shall be called..*
> *the house of prayer' but ye have made it"*...
> *a no smoking area.*

December 4th.

"Up betimes..."

... with everything to do. There was a last fragment of moon high in a troubled looking sky, and the usual owl noises, as I drew the curtains on what promised to be a tumultuous and troubled day.

No creature has a better sense of occasion that a horse, so, instead of trotting across the lane to the paddock, like animals heading in an orderly fashion up the gangway into the ark, they went to scatter up and down the lane, something they have never, ever, done before. Some drill-sergeant's language, and a lot of arm waving soon made them see sense.

Bringing them back to Chantry Mead an hour later I did something I

- 144 -

have been longing to attempt since Harvey arrived with us in May, led the three of them together, siblings in one hand, gooseberry in the other. It worked a treat. One day, when Diana isn't looking, I mean to try it from the saddle, when, if ever, we have three horses fit for work.

The next thing was to smuggle my notes into the pulpit, so that I might walk up the nave empty-handed come the time – I don't care to be seen carrying paper around, might be mistaken for a civil servant. Then there was the parking to be signed, and my parking squad to be deployed. It was a complicated plan, every square inch of hard-standing being in requisition, with countless cars expected and the ground so soft.

Our dear little church was, as expected, completely full, with much improvised seating and many having to stand. A farmer's funeral is always such a special gathering. Luckily I was on after the first hymn, so was not too long in 'the collecting ring', and, this time, had no problem being heard.

I had to quit the reception in the Village Hall early to be ready for Act II, the bit of the day I truly dreaded, getting Harvey into the vet hospital for his operation. They had no other in-patients, so there was nothing for it but to take Bella too. I feel quite desolate at leaving Dandy for weeks on his own, something I swore that I would never do: it's a betrayal of a herd animal. I took him a special treat, and made much of him, when we got back, but I can't forgive myself. I can hear him crying out for his sister now.

I shall not write another word, until I can write cheerfully. *Au revoir.*

XIV

"Use well the interval...".

January 30th, 2008.

IT'S over. After eight difficult weeks, at last, accompanied by the vet and his assistant we led the invalid and his duenna out of the stables, drugged and rubber-legged, to release them in Chantry Mead. Seeing them quietly grazing was a truly grateful sight. It was only matched by the sound of the low joyful whickering to each other of the brother and sister, when I brought Dandy, whom we had hidden away in Church Farm, also sedated, and released him in an adjoining portion of the meadow, whence he could safely commune with Bella over the fence.

Worse than the sheer drudgery of feeding, watering and tending to their beds around the clock, day in day out, was the burden on our minds of having the poor things un-naturally cooped up, with Dandy in solitary. Hearing our footsteps, they would invariably call to us, and we would go to any lengths to avoid passing within sight or earshot of the stables, unless it was to feed them.

Every day or so Bella had frantic, operatic, interludes, rushing round her box aimlessly; we had to sedate her. But Harvey was philosophical, quite the old soldier, knowing how lucky he was to find himself in a cushy billet; I have become really quite attached to him.

Dandy soon settled, gave no trouble, but seemed to welcome my company. On and off we spent quite a bit of time together. One occasion I particularly remember was, just after Christmas, I rode him up on Dungeon to find hounds, telling those I met that I was just checking on the legality of proceedings, as well as taking the opportunity to show them all what a really well-turned-out hunter looked like! Dandy was *au nature,* his mane in gorgon knots, as I delight to ride him when 'off duty' – he and I both disapprove of over-officious grooming.

As we came off the hill via Whitedown, its northerly field, I found myself hailed by a group of visitors from the Wilton (the South Dorset's Tuesdays draw people from all over). "Kitty's here!" they called out, naming a mare that I rode with that hunt a couple of seasons back. I have on the desk in front of me the shoe Kitty lost that day. A memento of a memorable morning, it frames a favourite picture of my undergraduate, 21-year-old father.

I left the hill in high conceit of myself at being thus recognised, you may be sure. Home, darkness falling, and hounds still speaking round about, we stood in the field shelter together, Dandy and I, he sniffing my pockets speculatively and rubbing his old face companionably against my shoulder. How I love that horse!

Another time, on the morning after getting back from our first visit of the skiing season to the Alps, I rode him up through Robert's wood to find that one of his old beeches had fallen across the track. It wasn't a big jump, but it was the last thing I wanted to face on a busy Monday morning when all I had in mind was to clear Park Lane of rubbish and get home. One couldn't shirk it, but he jumped hippo style, gracelessly, with a hump and a grunt, clearly not enjoying it, and reminding me of where we have got to in his life.

∽∾

THREE dramas had threatened the calm that we tried to maintain in our stable yard through Harvey's long convalescence: our fear was of him getting frightened or excited, and damaging the knee from which two quite large chips of bone had been so expensively extracted.

On one horrible morning Bella got cast in her box, rolling when I gave her some new bedding. Wedged on her back against the wall, nothing I could do would shift her. I tried first pulling this leg then that to roll her towards me, then getting purchase under her neck to lift her; all was futile. After a bit, as horses will, she seemed to give up, lay, very 'un-officerlike', rolling her eyes, doggo, resigned.

It was a terrifying nightmare, not the worst part being that I dare not call for help – Diana would never rest at the thought of Bella possibly casting herself again. (As I write, she still doesn't know of it).

At my wits' end, I at last thought to secure a rope round the hind fetlock ('ankle') furthest from me. Pulling with all my weight, and every ounce of strength that I could muster, I finally righted her. She staggered to her feet: I'm not sure which of us was the most shaken.

∽∾

THEN, on the morning of the last Sunday of the year, the Feast of the Holy Innocents, Diana, forbidden tennis and riding by the doctor and the vet, reduced to taking a walk for exercise, at a whim, looked in on the church to see how the Christmas flower arrangements were surviving. 'No Smoking' indeed: the place was in flames!

Within minutes four fire engines had answered her 999 call. The village was agog, but our concern was to stop the engines mistakenly coming up our drive and into the stable yard, and to beg the obliging firemen to switch off their sirens. Those same firemen reported that had Diana not discovered the fire when she did we would have lost the church.

As it is, we have lost the two rear pews in the de Glanville chapel, and the whole church interior is black and stinking. Under-floor electric wiring caused the fire: the parish is, fortunately, as Harvey is, well insured. I had hoped for at least a stained-glass window to commemorate Diana's feat, but have settled for a heap of brilliant firewood from the wreckage, and a length of moulded pew-back that I shall one day rejoice to find another use and a new life for. The PCC also, very generously, voted to give her a Garden Centre voucher; so we will have something else about the place in future years to remind us of that extraordinary morning.

The sad, charred fragments of oak, with their tight ancient joinery, burn wonderfully hot, and set one thinking. I, who cannot squeeze a lemon without wondering where it grew, find myself asking where did that acorn fall; when did it first spring into life; who felled the grown tree; who made those old pews; and did the hero of Blenheim rest some part of his young anatomy there when the Churchill family lived at Round Chimneys?

THE final drama came on the final day of the horses' long imprisonment, as I write, yesterday, the last vale-Tuesday of the season, when hounds met next-door at Church Farm. Having given both patients a mild sedative, and leaving Diana in charge, I went to help hand round drinks at the meet, and reluctantly to remind the Huntsman and Field Master, with due apologies, that we still had 'Do Not Disturb!' signs up in our yard. It goes against the grain to put even the slightest restriction on the hunt.

Diana needed to shop, we had only returned from a second short trip to the Alps the night before, so I was left with a watching brief, enjoined to hang around the stables until the hunt and all its usually so welcome music should clear the area. It seemed a good moment to prune brambles from a nearby hedge.

As I dragged a prickly faggot to the bonfire I was first electrified, then panic stricken, to see a fox making its unhurried, and I prayed un-hunted, way across the corner of our paddock, over the drive, disappearing into our neighbour's spinney. If it saw me it gave no sign of it: its 'line' ran no more than twenty paces from the stable door and Harvey's and Bella's all too alert faces. They were evidently as aware as I was of hounds speaking, uncertainly yet, but barely half a mile away: was there ever a better example of Murphy's Law?

You may be sure that I ran the 'heel line' (the way the fox had come) a great deal faster than that fox. A single hound was casting itself, giving tongue doubtfully, in 'far guzzle', as I call the distant end of Chantry Mead when we strip-graze it. It had given up and departed to rejoin the pack by the time I reached the old stile and gained the road, where Richard Tong, our Whipper-in, joined me. Breathless, I panted my concern that hounds should not run that line: he reassured me, he was just collecting stragglers, the pack had other business in hand.

DURING this long un-natural interval in our lives we escaped twice, briefly, as I have mentioned, to the Alps, twice I was allowed off the leash for a day to hunt down west, and I, once, fell in love.... with a hedge.

There is nothing, in my experience, quite so like being in love as laying a hedge (no coarse pun intended). Once you start at it, the hedge never quite leaves your mind, you go to bed, and wake, thinking of the next move... which uprights to discard, which save to lay, how to contrive to cover that thin bit, and so on, and so on?

When you are working there it completely engrosses and beguiles you, and, most valuable of all, forces its gentle pace on you. You cannot hurry, hedging: you must work with the wood: you forget time, until darkness falls, or duty calls. It says, as nothing else can....

"Be still my soul..."

... but this innocent love affair so nearly got me into trouble.

The days leading up to my hunting excursions are always anxious. Will the weather hold, will some misfortune intervene, will I get there – the drive is torture, I never expect a car to get me to my destination without it breaking down or involving me in an accident – until I'm safely in the saddle, and the photographer, usually and old friend, has greeted me, I can never quite believe the thing will actually come off?

On the very day before I was due out with the West Somerset I woke with a swollen wrist and a clumsy, stiff left hand. My hedging gauntlets having gone AWOL, I had been working in gardening gloves: a blackthorn had stabbed the inside of my wrist, to the bone.

Just a clean puncture, I had thought nothing of it at the time, but that morning it looked almost exactly like a horse's leg under the same injury, one that is all too common here in the Blackmore Vale. The stable remedy seemed appropriate, so I got Diana to apply an 'Animalintex' poultice. It worked like magic, immediately soothing the discomfort, and, by evening, drawing the wound, leaving the wrist and hand quite serviceable again.

⟡

MY swollen hand had focussed my mind on the signet ring my grand-mother had given me when she could no longer herself wear it. I can remember sealing letters for her with it when a small child – do people still seal letters? It bears the Muskett crest, that of the old Suffolk family that her mother, John Gould's daughter, married into.

The motto reads *Fide sed cui Vide*, faithful but with open eyes. It could scarcely be less appropriate for one who trusts on instinct, but I have become very attached to that ring. On the morning before the day with the West Somerset it threatened to have become all too firmly attached to me. How long before I, in my turn, will have to pass it on?

It is not only in opera and other fiction that rings, and the stones they bear, are credited with totemic powers. I read recently of several extraordinary instances of lost rings finding their owners, in one case after an interval of 67 years, and of a ring found in the sand on a beach a year after being lost.

My first wife, Gillian, once suddenly discovered that a treasured emerald had fallen from its ring setting. We were in Berlin, on the Maifeld, where Hitler used to stage grand shouting matches but where I was merely playing polo. It is a vast expanse of green – a needle in a haystack was nothing to an emerald supposed lost in all that grass. The stone was found sometime later, in the sweepings of the bathroom floor where we were staying.

My grandmother's ring once left me for several years. I had long since replaced it with a replica, or rather my insurance company had, when it came back to me though the post, found in a high cupboard that I had reached blindly up into when we were moving from a previous house on posting. In case you are wondering, I owned up to the insurance company: they kindly said "Forget it!".

February 3rd.

"Fiat lux"

CAN there be anything more purely white, or any sight more welcome, than the rump of a bullfinch exposed in flight? I haven't seen one of those loveliest of finches on our ground, or hardly anywhere, in ages: a pair fluttered out of the drive hedge as we returned from Castle Cary yesterday. I so hope that they are coming back, along with nuthatches, flycatchers and tree creepers, all once happily so commonplace round here.

The sight lightened my already lighter step. Having the three horses now comfortably re-settled in their outdoor life is like having a shackle struck suddenly from off my ankle: we are for Switzerland, *again*, tomorrow: I have the Cotley Harriers to look forward to on return: and it is Candlemas. Twenty-nine years ago, on this morning, Diana and I took ourselves off to get married in Richmond Registry Office: *fiat lux* indeed!

Intending to steal a march, last thing last night I crept down to the kitchen to put a card on the table. But there were two cards, back to back, propped on the pepper mill, when I came down for 'gunfire', ie to make the early mugs of tea. Diana's card to me had two lovey-dovey giraffes blowing kisses at each other, mine to her showed a filly meadow-romping with a carthorse. In the hope that you will say "Ah... h... h!", I give you the verse on its back...

"In the meadow you're companions, know how the rain feels.

With the sun on your back you can kick up your heels.
You can stand head to tail when the midges are out
And whisper just things that you both know about.
You'll call to each other on the days you're apart,
For each of you stays in the other one's heart."

February 9th.

"ARE you two to-ge-zaire?" asked the waitress; "Yes, we have been, for thirty years", I reply, with the slight exaggeration allowed to, indeed expected of, a journalist. We were sitting on the corners of two adjacent tables in the crowded *prêt-à-manger* at Geneva airport, the only oasis of any sanity and ease in that hell-on-earth.

We know the spot well, always head for it as the best place to pass the hours that must be wasted between coach and plane on the journey home from Verbier. To get there you have first to outwit the airport lift, surely the most stupid and disobliging lift in Europe. It is half-term, the airport is an anthill, but the waitress's pretty smile puts all to rights.

You won't want to read an account of yet another skiing holiday, they are all blissfully the same. The snow was perfect, there were no crowds to speak of, I fell only once – when a small, nicely mannered and apologetic child crashed into me. Best of all, the sun shone, you could see as well as feel the snow under your skis... I never had to use my new goggles, the ones I had found barely ten days before, abandoned on the floor in Zurich airport. (We went to St Moritz for a wedding; did I tell you?)

WAS that a blackbird or a thrush shouting *"De Rigueur!"* so imperiously as I fed the horses this morning? I shall lose my credibility as a countryman completely by confessing that I get them muddled, but I do. Some years ago I wrote an unbelievably clever article settling the matter for ever, invented an unforgettable way of sorting one little songster from the other, but I can't remember what it was, and have no idea where to look for the piece among eighteen un-indexed scrapbooks of my waiting-room fodder.

Oh Well! It was a thrush... or a blackbird... we'll have to leave it at that.... but no, it has just come back to me. It's in the punctuation. A blackbird inquires, gently, poetically, there is always a query in his tone, and a question-mark at the end of all his strophes. A thrush is much more peremptory. As this morning, he issues commands, his every phrase ending with an exclamation mark. The next time you hear one, see if I'm not right.

"HOW do I buy something, please!?" I called out plaintively whilst shopping in Boots recently. One 'attendant' had her head in a file of papers far off at the end of a long, empty counter, another, bottom in the air, had hers in a draw equally distant at the other end. The bespectacled Dispenser, Apothecary, or Alchemist, or whatever he is called, had more important things to do than sell things to customers (fair enough, haven't I often been grateful for his prompt, kindly, undivided attention and helpful, expert advice?).

I was eventually gently put in my place by the girl with her head buried in papers. "I've got to finish this before the man comes for the photographs", she said in response to my pathetic bleat, but relented sufficiently to relieve me of the usual £20 of so that it costs to get in and out of Boots with Diana's shopping list.

It seems a long time since the customer was king: the purchaser is all too often a petitioner these days, and nowhere more so than at airports. But there are plenty of old-fashioned shops still in Sherborne I'm happy to say.

I made two resolutions on this particular shopping expedition. That, when I am really old, I will try not to drop anchor suddenly, without warning, in shop doorways or on busy pavements, and that I will do my best not to look cross the whole time. No doubt both resolutions are easier made than kept, and I shall, in my turn, fail in both departments.

My reference to airports relates to recent experience. Even at Bournemouth, which, in scale and helpfulness, knocks spots off any other of our airports that I know, on a slow day, with few passengers, we are still put through superfluous taped chicanes in order to reach the all-important officials who need to inspect our documents or baggage. It must be fun for them watching us zigzag hectically hither and thither towards them, as though we were enjoying some sort of round dance, not participating in that most stressful and tiring of modern rituals, air-travel, and paying for the privilege.

It would take the airport staff all of half a minute to dismantle the wretched things temporarily when traffic is light, and would have the great advantage of showing that they had some thought for our comfort and convenience. If I bleat at Boots, I sometimes feel like bellowing "Moo!" at airports, where one is all too often treated like market cattle, except that the RSPCA would never allow such needless cruelty.

WE HAVE been having the most terrific sunrises and sunsets these recent days. Very confusing it must be for shepherds: are they to be delighted or take warning? In fact the weather has been beautiful, if arctic, the horses walk gingerly on concrete, and breaking the ice on their trough requires more muscle each succeeding Eskimo day.

This morning, first thing, I was stopped in my tracks by the sight of our poor ravaged church, seen through the easterly window of my mother's old room, standing tall against an enormous flaming orange background. You could see the glow actually piercing the bell tower wall to wall through its 'ears', its open tracery.

I suddenly realised that we, in this dear old house, are the only people in whole the world who have that precise and precious view, and thought of all those rectors, their early-rising servants and their families enjoying it, over past centuries.

Another, less serious, thought, was that the colour of the morning sky was exactly that of a Ralph Lauren shirt that I bought in 'Drat the Children' in Sherborne, before our last skiing trip. I call the charity shop at the top of Cheap Street 'Drat the Children' because it is always tempting me off the straight and narrow, I haven't paid so much for a shirt since carefree Jermyn Street days of long ago. It cost £12.50, a ridiculous extravagance, but I couldn't resist the thought of astonishing Diana with it.

It was slightly deflating, when we flew out of Bournemouth a few days later, to discover that its brilliant flaming orange hue precisely matched that of the Easyjet cabin-staff livery.

Febuary 25th.

"When all at once I saw…"

STARTING with a game of 'dodge the parson', closing with our winning 52p in tuppenny points at bridge, betweenwhiles acquiring a new horse, getting into an embarrassing muddle over Flora, attending a brilliant party, and perhaps best of all, learning some good news about farming, yesterday was an extraordinary day.

Three sparrows were squabbling viciously in the lower branches of the lime tree, oblivious of me, within arm's reach, as I walked the saddle out through the shrubbery to Chantry Mead. *"Cherchez la femme"* I thought: all the garden birds seem to be well into their courting season.

Bella and I had a job to do. I find that I just cannot bring myself to attend 'church' services in the Village Hall, and have been gently taken to task for it. They're right of course, it shows the superficiality of my religious faith; I ought to go willingly to church wherever services are being held.

The point was made, although I didn't need telling, that the PCC needed its regular 'collection' income, so, whilst my friend Michael was driving by Kennels Lane to his Sunday morning duties, Bella and I took the cross-country route through Hay Wood to his neighbour's, the PCC Treasurer's house, to slip a conciliatory and repentant cheque through his letter-box.

OUT of the wood, twinkletoes skipped nimbly over a fallen branch: it was nothing, and she made nothing of it, but she has the most lovely natural jump... if only she had the nerve to go with it. She was soon to remind me of the other side of her nature.

Emerging from fording the Caundle Brook, we saw, mid-field ahead of us, a female figure, apparently measuring out the ground with a drill sergeant's pace-stick (a massive pair of dividers), being circled by an excited spaniel, which soon switched its red-Indian war-dance attentions to Bella.

It was the wife of the grazing tenant of the land we were crossing, one of whose Jersey heifers I had reported as being in trouble some months back, as she gratefully recalled when I introduced myself. She told me of their widespread farming interests, how dairy farming was at last looking up – as I could hardly until then believe, although I had read of it – how they had 'gone organic', that it had been a good move, their milk sold well.

She was 'measuring the grass' she told me, having broken off, making a brief pencilled note, to speak to me. She showed me the cuts in the turf where they had injected some manure, so as not to sour the grass by putting it on the surface. "We have a lovely life" she said, "and it's so good for our two boys, being out in the country, instead of loafing around wondering what to do with themselves". "Will they go into farming?" I asked, and got the answer I expected. "Neither of my sons are soldiers" I said as we parted, "and I'm not a doctor".

All in all it was one of the pleasantest chance encounters I have had in months, and the best news I have heard in years. It would have been a different story, I suppose, had I met a pig or sheep farmer.

❧

WHEN we quit my new friend, Bella suddenly went ape. I just could not get her to focus on the gate, which, off one hinge, could not be shut without her usual intelligent practical co-operation. Instead she fixed a petrified gaze on the receding figure of the lady with the 'pace-stick' – she has a horror of distant, unintelligible movement. Neither the circling dog nor the pacing 'drill-sergeant' had disturbed her equanimity before, but now, quite irrationally, as they disappeared over the crest of the field, the sight set her alight.

There was nothing for it but to dismount to secure the gate, and no possibility of immediately getting into the saddle again. I almost forgot the purpose of our errand, as, downright dangerous in her sudden barging movements, and circus antics, we gained Tiley, the small hamlet in the fields, where my father used occasionally to visit his patients on horseback, and where the our Treasurer lives.

The storm passed, as it always does with Bella, and soon she was her gentle, biddable, adorable self again, as bright as a button, as good a hack as I ever rode. But do you wonder that I won't let Diana ride her?

"… the happy highways where I went and cannot come again."

WE were invited to lunch at the Countryside Alliance point-to-point at Badbury Rings, and, on a whim, I took the old route to Blandford, over Bulbarrow: with the roads so narrow, and the climb so steep, it's not really the sensible way to go. I soon wished that I hadn't. The state of long stretches of those old familiar lanes, strewn with rubbish, was heart-breaking. I just don't know which I find more difficult to fathom, the shamelessness of those who litter, or the lack of pride, or any sense of ownership, on the part of the people who live, but are content to leave it lying, there.

Stoke Lane, beyond Mappowder, too narrow to be a rat-run, and thus much as I remember it, is a part of the old road from Sherborne to Milton Abbas, it would have been busy with monkish traffic through the middle ages. When I first knew it there was a ford, now bridged, where it crosses a tributary of the Lydden. My father told me that a carter and his horse, homebound at night, were once swept away and drowned at that place. You'd believe it if you have seen how angry, quick and dangerous the harmless-looking Lydden can become after sudden heavy rain.

Apart from the Flora fiasco, Badbury Rings was a joy. I didn't see much of the racing, the lunch was too good, the situation too beguiling. I could prop myself against the outside of Strutt & Parker's pavilion, attentive hosts brought me food and drink, old, familiar, comfortable, hunting friends talked to me, and the whole doggy, tweedy crowd surged by under my, as ever, speculative eye.

⤜∾⤐

THE Flora thing was like a comic opera plot, except that it didn't have a happy ending. Amongst the e-mail rubbish waiting for me when we returned from one of our recent Swiss trips was a message from my friend, the Editor of *Horse & Hound*, saying that a mare called Flora was looking for kindly home. I bit; Flora's keeper responded positively; then silence, quite a long silence (all this on e-mail, I never telephone anybody if it can be avoided)… nobody's fault, as I later learnt, Flora and co were moving house.

In the interval a conditional offer of another horse to be homed came up, Ollie, he sounded very promising. Flora seemed to have vanished, so we agreed to have Ollie, should his owner like the idea… again silence. A complication that you need to be aware of is that Diana rather favoured Ollie, whose connections were old friends of hers, and was inclined to be down on the outsider Flora, whom I rather fancied.

This was the situation when we got to Badbury Rings, if you have followed the plot so far: Flora was to be forgotten, Ollie was a possibility, but

– 155 –

no more. As I advanced on lunch, my arm was seized and my hand shaken by a personable stranger who introduced herself as Flora's friend, "Was I still interested?" she asked. I said "Yes!", subject only to another proposition that we were committed to but were by no means sure of, not materializing. I agreed to visit, ride Flora, fixed a day even.

Meanwhile Diana had steamed on lunch-wards, unaware of my encounter, by chance met Ollie's 'mother', been handed a very handsome photograph of him, clinched the deal, he's to be delivered by the week-end. I leave you to guess the rest of the story.

On the way home, Diana driving – again, I leave you to guess why – and on the sensible route, a carpet of the most brilliant yellow in the little spinney by Dark's Bridge caught the eye. "Primroses?" I queried; my driver, who has a better eye than me, demurred.

HENTY, as I call the robin who so often is in evidence, seen or heard, by the paddock gate when I have business with the horses, was flitting around, brazenly, almost in reach, as I gave Bella her feed after riding her this morning. She is a touch under weight after her long incarceration 'matron' says, after putting a tape-measure round all their girths, and gets supplementary grub after work. Henty, flirting the white feather in his wing, hops around all hopeful; he reckons that there is something in it for him.

Bella and I have just been to check on those 'primroses', and found...

"... a crowd,
A host of golden daffodils."

February 27th.

SORRY to go on about birds, but just now they really force themselves on one's attention. That thrush, after laying down the law again this morning, moved on to shouting a manic "Emu! Emu! Emu!", followed by "Quick! Quick! Quick!" – as if I needed telling. Diana has a girls' lunch-eon party; my appointed role is to feed the horses early, light a fire in the big room, get Jasper to Hazlegrove for ten-past-eight, and then make myself scarce for the day.

Jasper is great company, and I wanted to talk to him, to try somehow to explain the historical oddness of the coincidence that has his mother in Ho Chi Mihn City for the *Daily Mail,* and her stepbrother, at the same time, in Pyongyang, for *Associated Press.* Miles is getting pictures for the viewing world of the historic visit to North Korea of the New York Philharmonic Orchestra: Mel is re-visiting scenes of her childhood with her father, who was a military attaché there during the Vietnam war.

I was defeated in my, probably impossible, purpose by the wireless: the Third Programme was playing a recording of Mozart's 3rd Horn Concerto. The second movement is just too beautiful to allow of anything but rapt attention... that and driving safely of course. I feel an almost terrifying sense of responsibility when I have Jasper for a passenger.

"See you at three-thirty" were his parting words: I am to watch him captain the under-ten hockey B team against Millfield Prep.

MY PLAN was to follow Mel's example and re-visit childhood scenes, in Devon. It didn't answer, in fact, barring one scene, it was a mistake. Nothing was as I remembered it; no-one I met had a memory going back to the 1940s; the farm we lodged at, where I learnt to milk a cow, saw cider made, and became a country boy, was all barn conversions, no trace of cider orchards let alone a cow. My school was a nursing home, where, hovering, uncertain on its gravel sweep, where we used to do PT, I was driven off by the sound from somewhere indoors of a miserable, demented cry.

The one success was visiting the tiny church at Buckerell, west of Honiton, which we schoolchildren attended. The door at the foot of the tower looked locked, but wasn't; the interior, with its box pews and rood screen was just as I remembered it, and it provided me with a moment, and a memory, that made the long drive, the whole day, utterly worth while.

I was seven years old in 1940, when I first went to join my brother at his school. It was the winter term, and, the first time in my life that I was singled out from among my peers, I was to read a lesson at the carol service. We weren't able to rehearse in church, but the mistress who coached me said that she would mark the start and end of my lesson in pencil in the lectern bible so that I would have no difficulty finding it.

Have you guessed? When I opened the old bible at the first page of the New Testament, there, faint but discernible, were her pencil marks of all but seventy years ago. I re-read the lesson to the empty church, trying for a few moments to re-enter my war-time Devon childhood, remember my mother, for whom those times must have been so very tough, sitting proudly in the congregation, and my father, away somewhere on the perilous high seas.

Beautifully expressed, the well-remembered passage contains wording and notions that must have been puzzling to a child, but were no doubt explained to me. I think of it as one of the loveliest passages in the most beautiful book in our language.

"Now the birth of Jesus Christ was on this wise..."

March 1st.

I WAS up at sunrise on my Saint's Day, having been miserable company out to supper on the previous evening, and barely slept through a long wakeful night. Expected at teatime, with generous daylight in hand, my new horse Ollie had arrived as darkness fell. We had been very doubtful about the wisdom of doing so, but there was nothing for it but to introduce him to his new companion, Dandy, and new grazing when, humans anyway, could barely see. We were so worried that he might injure himself on unfamiliar ground in the inevitable high jinks and excitement, not to mention crash into strange, perhaps dimly seen, fencing.

With the dawn there was half a waning moon hanging, still high, in the cloudless southern sky, and a strong warm, westerly gale blowing – I won't mention the birdsong. I found the two geldings companionably grazing in the distant corner of 'far guzzle', by the old pond, the gable end of the village's lovely 'Saxon' farmhouse a backdrop.

As soon as he saw me, Ollie strode purposefully my way – just what I had hoped for – better even, as well as being man-friendly, he was sound... and so was Dandy... and so were Bella and Harvey across the fence. We had got away with it.

Ollie is a handsome, sixteen-hand-plus, bay crossbred, of a little, but not much, less than Dandy's age, and with an impressive hunting record, first with the Beaufort, then the Taunton Vale. A slight tendon injury before Christmas ruled him out as a young thruster's horse: I have promised not to take him over any big drop fences (!). He just needs a loving home and gentle hunting. It all seems too good to be true.

And, in case you are wondering about the 'Saxon' farmhouse, that's also a bit of a fairy story. Some few years back, the then owner of Chantry Cottage, which looks across the road into our meadow, had a fancy to build an extension. It is a frame-house, very reminiscent of the vernacular farm architecture of northern Germany, and did something I would have rated impossible... improved our lovely corner of Dorset.

DANDY has sorted out who is boss in Chantry Mead, he wouldn't let Ollie near the hay-rack when I filled it at tea-time. As always, I had put half the ration in the shelter, but it was a problem showing this to Ollie. Having nothing to lead him with but the binder-twine in my pocket, I put that round his neck, and he followed me lamb-like. If he jumps timber for me, and keeps sound, I really think he will prove to be a dream come true. On Monday, Duffy will shoe him, I'll get a saddle on him and see what he's like to ride.

March 6th.

"WHATEVER you do, don't smoke", I said to Jasper as I fixed the ring in his nose; it was a fractured leather washer from my mower petrol can. It is 'World Book Day', he has to appear at school as a character from a favourite book, and has chosen to be the bull that features in *CIA Cows in Action* by Steve Cole.

His horns are sharpened sections form the broken bowed back of a Windsor chair, proving the rule 'never throw wood away'; they are seated on a poll of sheep-hide, secured under his chin with knicker-elastic; his tail is a hank of rope, and, as he disappears to join his class-mates, a large sign on his back reads "Moo!".

Fixing the horns was no simple job, I broke two twist drills doing it, when they fouled, first the wool, then the elastic (handymen of either sex will understand), the whole thing occasionally whirling round in the most alarming and slightly dangerous fashion. I nearly got myself gored.

But Jasper's and my carpentry is not all one-sided. A few days later, when, with typical kindness, he and his mother turned up for supper on my birthday, Jasper put a surprise present into my hands, my eyes tight shut of course. It was little wooden gadget of uncertain purpose.

When I asked what it was he looked at me in that pitying way children have for slow-minded adults. "It's a 'per'" he said. Sure enough, it was, obviously, a letter 'P' carved in wood. He'd done it in woodwork class that afternoon he told me. All my 'steppies' call me Peppie.

March 13th, 2008.

"The Last Ride Together"

I HAD hoped to hunt somewhere today, but couldn't wangle it. Then I settled in my mind for having a last ride on Dandy, but, for one reason or another, ended up riding all three horses. I don't think that I have ever done that before, except once, out hunting... ridden three horses in one day.

I had to take Bella out to accompany Harvey, who must be worked before the vet should inspect him, and see how lame he still is. It's a sad story, and I won't burden you with it. Suffice it to say that we seem to have come near the end of the road with that little horse. We have both become very fond of him. Diana was in tears when the vet shook his head.

I rode Ollie later, because we needed eggs, and anyway I can't resist riding him, each day one day less of the six weeks I am sentenced to keeping him in slow work. He is a gorgeous, lively ride. The only problem is dismounting. His head-carriage is so high that I find it quite a labour clearing the crest of his mane with a forward swinging leg – I've always got off in that unorthodox fashion, 'the wrong way', since quitting the Pony Club and riding school.

Ollie showed a bit of character at the egg farm, wouldn't approach the gate, backed off, apparently terrified – doesn't like the smell of goats I guess. Rather than have a row, I did what I always do with a nappy horse, got off and led him. My guess is that he'll be more sensible next time: they usually are.

∽∾

DANDY had been more-or-less sound as I rode him up to Robert's wood first thing, and he jumped the fallen tree quite in his old style – no pregnant hippo today. It was as if he were saying "What's the fuss, there's nothing whatever wrong with me!".

Two roe danced away from us, flaunting their powder-puff tails, and the whole wood was full of song, with a woodpecker on drums. I used to think that that hammering was the bird digging for insects until I learnt that in fact it is the cock greater-spotted marking out his territory, and, at this season, perhaps advertising for a mate – part of Nature's lonely hearts column.

Out in the open, Dandy stumbled, badly, four times as we crossed the deep going at the foot of Dungeon. But in Park Lane, and off his back, he followed me in his usual endearing way, hands off, stopping and coming on at a word. I shall have his shoes off next time Duffy comes. At least he can summer with us. Dear, dear old Dandy; what a precious part of my life his life has been; it will be 17 years this May that, one teatime, to the admiration of our neighbours, Daisy dropped him in our paddock.

"For the means of grace, and for the hope of glory."

WHAT does grace, my mother's name, mean? I once sat through a sermon on just that subject, a good sermon, but ended up none the wiser. I reckon it to be a part of Alice's vocabulary, it means what I want it to mean. For me grace is what we all strive for, to live a life of which we need not be entirely ashamed. Displaying 'grace when under pressure' is to my mind the best description of how a soldier should strive to behave.

I love this place, which I was brought to as a boy... our house, this hill, everything in view of it, and beyond, especially to the west. I think it no shame to love the land I was born in, to hold it dearer, and think it better than any other country in the world, to revere its history, and, almost above all, its gift to humanity, its precious language.

Seventy-five years ago this morning my mother, a young doctor's wife, gave birth to her third child, her second son, and named him after the hero of a book she had just been reading. My father was then a houseman at St Thomas's.

As for glory in this life, when I was a boy I thought to conquer the world, as a young man would have settled for a field marshal's baton, and then, at last, I hope, grew up, grateful to find a few things within my competence that I could usefully do.

We are swamped daily with news of far-flung disasters, invited to emote over what we cannot possibly ameliorate, let alone mend. For myself, I think the answer is to do what seems to need doing and is within reach... which is why I try my best to be a good neighbour... and, amongst other things, why I was off Dandy's back this morning, when we quit Dungeon Hill and entered on Park Lane – which is where you and I met up again, and where I finally leave you. From the bottom of my heart, thank you for your company. Dear reader, good night and goodbye.

"Oh sweet and blessed country..."

The Ragbag
(Quotations cross-referenced to the pages they appear on.)

Page 9 – Full marks if you can guess where this tiny scrap comes from! It is from the opening pages of Thomas Hardy's *The Return of the Native*. As with so many of his books, he starts his story with a central character travelling a Dorset lane – such a clever way of parachuting the reader straight into the plot, and into his beloved 'Wessex'.

Pages 9 & 16 –This comes from *The Knight's Tale*, by Geoffrey Chaucer (c1345-1400). I first met it in my 5th Form English class at Clifton, aged I suppose 15 or 16, under a brilliant teacher called Major, I didn't know his first name, one didn't in those days, Gee. It struck me then, and it stays with me now, as a wonderful evocation of life's ups and downs, its bright sunlight and its deep shadows. A hand of friendship and of consolation held out to the lonely by one of the earliest artists in our peerless language, here is the whole verse...

> *"What is this world? What asketh men to have?*
> *Now with his love, now in his colde grave,*
> *Allone, with-outen any companye".*

Page 17 – Back to school again! This is part of the famous passage from Eccesliastes11 that starts "Remember now thy Creator in the days of thy youth...", a completely wasted bit of advice in my experience! However, as you can see, I have remembered it, the lesson read every year at 'Commem'. In context it reads...

> *"Or ever the silver cord be loosed, or the golden bowl*
> *be broken, or the pitcher be broken at the fountain,*
> *or the wheel at the cistern".*

The novelist Henry James was evidently struck by this passage too.

Page 21 – From *The Deserted Village*, a great favourite, and surely a text for our time?

Page 22 – From *David Copperfield*, after whom I was named my mother used to claim; she was reading it whilst she was carrying me. I'm rather ambivalent about Charles Dickens, loved him until I met Jane Austen, who has a gentler touch and tells things as they were.

Page 23 – Shakespeare at last, and Hamlet of course, from the great soliloquy in Act III. First met, at least first strongly taken on board, in Olivier's film version, and then, most unforgettably, at the Edinburgh Festival, with Richard Burton and Claire Bloom.

Page 24 – *King Lear I iv.*

Page 24 – From the opening chapter of *The Return of the Native*, written by Thomas Hardy at a happy interlude in his life, early in his first marriage, when living at Sturminster Newton. He thought it (and I think it), his best novel.

Page 25 – This comes from *Boswell's Life of Samuel Johnson*, the entry carries the date April 10th, 1778. My copy, an abbreviated edition illustrated, delightfully, by Ernest Shepard, was given me by my father when I was 17 years old. I read every word of it, the great Doctor has stood not far from my shoulder ever since.

Page 29 – From Tennyson's *The Charge of the Light Brigade*: the 13th Light Dragoons were a Balaklava regiment.

Page 29 – From John of Gaunt's deathbed speech of course, phrases from which for ever crop up in my mind, *Richard II 1 iii*.

Page 35 – The first film I ever remember seeing as a child was Walt Disney's *Snow White*: I must have been no more than six, but I think of it as one of the best films I ever saw, this is from the heroine's charming song.

Page 38 – Is there a more crushingly poignant last scene in any of Shakespeare's Tragedies? I suppose that this one has a special message for soldiers, I think I like it best, but then I only have to glance at one of the others to throw myself into doubt, *Othello 5 ii*.

Page 41 – The first line of a Great War song that was still popular in my nursery days, the 1930s.

Page 44 – *Hamlet 4 vii*.

Page 44 – Being 'close mewed up' was what happened to poor Clarence before he got tipped head-first into a malmsey butt - *Richard III 1 i*.

Page 45 - This long quote is from *Hillingdon Hall* by RS Surtees, the last of the three Jorrocks novels, least known but, to my mind, almost the best.

Page 50 – From Thomas Hardy's *Far From the Madding Crowd*, Ch II.

Page 51 – Housman, a poet whose work I was devoted to for a short while as a young man, this gem is from *More Poems,* and is number xxxvi. His dates were 1859-1936, like Binyon (see below) he lived and wrote through the tragic shadows of WWI with its massive casualties.

Pages 53, 57 & 59 – From Laurence Binyon's *Poems for the Fallen*. What a thing, to have written such lapidary lines, spoken all over the world year after year! His dates were 1869-1943, what can have been his thoughts as we embarked on World War II? *(Since these words are for ever quoted in service sheets I hope that there are no copyright implications to my borrowing them. I applied formally to the Binyon Estate for permission, but no answer came.)*

Page 56 – *Eheu* comes from Horace I am told, and is Latin for Ah me! I rather like the word.

Page 56 – From *Isaiah,* or so I thought until I came to look for it. If you ever sung in Handel's Messiah these words must surely always be set to music in your mind, his librettist, Charles Jennens (1700–1773) is due some of the credit.

Page 57 - another favourite bit from Othellos's fine, final speech *Act V ii*.

Page 58 – *Ecclesiastes 44 vii.*

Page 58 Robert Graves, the title of his 1929 autobiography.

Page 60 - *Acts 9 xviii.*

Page 60 – Hardy again, from *The Return of the Native.*

Page 61 - Rudyard Kipling, the soldier's poet, from *Tomlinson.*

Page 64 – *The Last of the Mohicans* by James Fenimore Cooper, and *Moonfleet* by James Meade Falkner.

Page 69 – I wonder how many can place this tag? It's French for April Fool of course, but the words head up a chapter in *The Experiences of an Irish RM* by Edith Somerville and her cousin Martin Ross, a book especially dear to me. My father asked me to read to him from it when I last saw him.

Page 78 – The title of a book by Grey of Fall'odon.

Pages 80&81 – *Richard III 3 iii.*

Page 81 – *Luke 15.*

Page 87 – *Hamlet* again, *Act 1 v.*

Page 92 – Dr Johnson, as reported by Boswell, for once talking rubbish!

Page 93 – More *Hamlet,* the Prince speaking disrespectfully to Polonius in *Act 2 ii.* I remember my father telling me that it was no way in which to speak to an old man, however foolish.

Page 95 - *Hamlet* yet again, almost the opening lines. Anybody who has ever done guard duty will know exactly what Francisco meant, it's absolute misery.

Page 99 – *"The Grand old Duke of York..."*; need I go on?

Pages 99 – *Julius Caesar Act 1 ii.*

Page 101 – I don't know where this, so useful, invocation comes from, was it a song, or the title of a musical?

Page 102 – The whole delightful nonsense couplet by Christopher Isherwood goes *'The common cormorant (or shag)/Lays its eggs inside a paper bag'.* (reproduced with permission of Curtis Brown Group Ltd, London, on behalf of the estate of Christopher Isherwood. Copyright Christopher Isherood, 1966.)

Page 106 – From Flanders and Swann's brilliant *The Gas Man Cometh.*

Page 108 – This is a cheat, and I apologise for it. The phrase, suddenly naming my own regiment, and making me sit up sharp, doesn't appear in *Bleak House.* The words are put into the mouth of Lady Dedlock in the TV version.

Page 109 – *Pomp & Circumstance* of course, but did you know that the words were by AC Benson? I didn't until I looked them up.

Page 112 – The title of one of Hardy's earliest and happiest books, quoting from *As You Like It Act II v.*

Page 115 – King Henry IV, Part I Act IV ii.

Page 118 – *Love's Labour's Lost, Act V ii,* the next line, as you no doubt remember, is suggestively hilarious "While greasy Joan doth keel the pot", & *Richard II, Act II i.*

Page 121 – Thomas Hardy's *The Woodlanders* Ch 29; 'Newton Buckton' is of course Buckland Newton.

Page 127 – *Antony & Cleopatra, Act V ii.*

Page 129 – *Alice in Wonderland Ch 11.*

Page 130 – *I Kings XVIII v44.*

Page 131 – This is Lord Scamperdale blowing up Mr Sponge in *Mr Sponge's Sporting Tour* by RS Surtees.

Page 135 – Anthony Trollope's *Barchester Towers Ch VI;* a bit naughty this, but brevity seems to be the one thing that they do not teach at theological colleges.

Page 137 – From Kipling's powerful, prophetic and widely misunderstood poem *Recessional.* It has a date on it, June 22nd 1897, the day of Queen Victoria's Diamond Jubilee, & a couplet from *Ode to a Nightingale* by Keats.

Page 138 – Kipling again, from *Collected Dog Stories.*

Page 140 – The opening line of Shaw's *Saint Joan.*

Page 142 – *Julius Caesar V iii.*

Page 144 – *Mark 11 xvii,* & a Samuel Pepys diary entry June 9th, 1666.

Page 146 – From Cardinal Newman's *The Dream of Gerontius,* so wonderfully set to music by Elgar. My parents adored 'The Dream', and so do I.

Page 149 – This plangent line comes from the words set, in the year of my birth, to a melody in Sibelius's *Finlandia,* they echo a line from Housman's *A Shropshire Lad.*

Page 150 – I don't pretend to be a Latin scholar, but *fiat lux* of course means "Let there be light", which phrase forms the last line in all the verses of a favourite Candlemas hymn. Could you have better examples of the beautiful brevity of two great languages, I wonder how the phrase comes out in German!?

Page 150 – The verse is by Mary Lascelles, it comes from her 'Village Life'.

Page 153 &156 – Worsdworth, of course!

Page 155 – AE Houseman, from *A Shropshire Lad, xxxix.*

Page 157 – Matthew 1 xviii-xxiii.

Page 159 – The title of a poem by Robert Browning.

Page 160 – From A General Thanksgiving in the Book of Common Prayer.

Page 161 –A line from Hymn 278, 'Jerusalem the Golden', perhaps my favourite of all Hymns A&M. Bernard of Cluny, the 12th century Burgundian monk, wrote the words, which were translated from the Latin by James Mason Neale (1818-1866), and so delightfully set to music by A.Ewing (1830-1895).

GWALB

Will you become a member of GWALB? It costs nothing, and if you join you can put the letters after your name in official correspondence, your letters to Buckingham Palace etc (only kidding)! GWALB stands for Glanvilles Wootton Against Litter Bugs.

Seriously, I think it would be so sad just to let our bit of Dorset sink under a sea of litter. This is what I picked up this morning coming down Park Lane (the road from Buckland Newton) today, in less than a mile…

1, sort of, face flannel
15 pages of 'Trade It' – tastefully spread through the mile
1 Coke bottle & 3 razor-sharp, flattened Coke tins
8 chocolate etc wrappers & 1 sweet paper
1 milk container & 3 plastic bottles
1 crisp packet & 5 fag packets
9 pieces of litter that you wouldn't thank me for describing.

It's just a week since I last cleared Park Lane, so does this mean that every year 52 face flannels, 208 Coke cans/bottles… 468 various pieces etc will be left lying there when I turn my toes up? Is this what we want?

I realise that many reading this don't have the leisure I do as a self-employed person, busy young mums, those working 9 – 5, but I beg those of my neighbours who do have the chance, and perhaps have a daily route through the parish, to help on a regular basis with picking up rubbish.

Would you PLEASE be prepared to take on or share responsibility for one of the pitches in the attached list? If you would be so very kind as to return it to me I will make a plan, and tell everybody who is doing what.

Picking up litter seems thankless, and unending, but I am sure that, like broken windows and graffiti in towns, litter breeds litter, and the effort pays off. If there is something too large, heavy or horrible, like the badger I picked up on Monday, do give me a ring and I'll deal with it.

Saturday, 10th September 2005.   David Edelsten GWALB.